Beloved Land

A RICHARD JEFFERIES ANTHOLOGY

Beloved Land

A RICHARD JEFFERIES ANTHOLOGY
EDITED BY *Colin McKelvie*
ILLUSTRATED BY *Esdaile Hudson*

SWAN·HILL
PRESS

Copyright © 1994 by Colin McKelvie (Introduction), Esdaile Hudson (illustrations)

First published in the UK in 1994
by Swan Hill Press
an imprint of Airlife Publishing Ltd

British Library Cataloguing in Publication Data
A catalogue record for this book
is available from the British Library

ISBN 1 85310 421 3

Printed in England by Livesey Ltd., Shrewsbury

Swan Hill Press
an imprint of Airlife Publishing Ltd.
101 Longden Road, Shrewsbury SY3 9EB, England

Contents

Introduction

RICHARD JEFFERIES was a unique author. The critical labels and pigeon-holes that commentators and historians of literature find so convenient occasionally fail to provide a comfortable and adequate niche for an individual writer. Predetermined categories cannot always accommodate authors whose particular gifts and achievements are oblique or multifaceted, or whose quirky individualism indicates a restlessly enquiring mind and an ability to range widely across disciplines and philosophies that may often appear exclusive and distinctive. Richard Jefferies is usually described as a 'country writer', a vague and ill-defined category at best, and one that does not do justice to the full breadth of Jefferies' writings and personal interests. As a professional journalist whose living depended upon the satisfaction of his readers and editors, he combined a useful versatility and the good journalist's ability of acquiring a command of a subject quickly — and of writing about it with fluent assurance — with a disposition that was restless, questioning and widely informed. He could write with enthusiasm and considerable technical understanding about technological matters, and there is more than a hint of High Victorian confidence in his pieces on the development of the railways, the proliferation of trade, and the emergence of new machinery and newly-evolving philosophies of manufacturing and agriculture. He wrote and published a number of novels, a genre in which he had hoped to specialise but which was ill-suited to his particular gifts as a reporter and essayist.

Jefferies first came to public prominence in 1872, at the age of twenty-four, with a detailed letter to *The Times* on the pay and conditions of farm labourers in Wiltshire, and it is for his writings on the countryside, farming, wildlife, field sports and rural communities that he has always been best-remembered and most highly regarded since his death in 1887 at the early age of thirty-eight. A career in journalism, first on the staff of regional newspapers in Gloucestershire and Wiltshire and then as a freelance feature writer and novelist, led him to live within easy reach of London, successively in Surrey, Kent and Sussex. But his roots were deep in the countryside (he was brought up on a small family farm in north Wiltshire, near Swindon) and the bulk of his finest writing had a country setting and treats of country creatures and occupations. The geographical gamut of his best work encompasses landscapes from Somerset to Kent, an English region that he knew intimately: Jefferies is pre-eminently a writer about the southernmost parts of England, seldom extending his scope north of the Thames.

Meadow Thoughts dates from April 1884 and contains some of Jefferies' best descriptions of both a broad sweep of landscape and the intimacies of small details seen and heard. It is also a powerful expression of the feelings that he had struggled to explain earlier in *The Story of My Heart*, Jefferies' 'autobiography of the soul' that had been published in October 1883; his sense of rapt wonder at natural things, of joys in all life, when 'an inexpressible thought quivered in the azure overhead . . . the very grass blades confounded the wisest, the tender lime leaf put them to shame . . .' He acknowledges his own frustrated sense of the futility of attempting to describe these profundities of feeling: 'the very shade of the pen on the paper tells you how hopeless it is to express these things', for paper can never be an adequate 'mind-tablet'. In this he is perhaps indirectly acknowledging the failure of what he had tried to achieve in *The Story of My Heart* and his other mystical writings, where his skills as a writer and his usual mastery of words falter and fail when confronted with 'thoughts and imaginings . . . too deep to be written'.

In these late summer thoughts he expresses his sense of the wild profusion and infinitely rich fecundity of Nature – 'prodigality and superfluity are stamped on everything she does' – compared with the 'littleness, and meanness, and niggardliness forced upon us by our circumstances'. It is a theme to which he returned at greater length, using many of the same turns of phrase, in a piece of writing which remained in manuscript at the time of his death, and was not eventually published until 1948 under the title *The Old House at Coate*. Chapter eight of this is entitled 'The Prodigality of Nature and Niggardliness of Man', and the longer text of which it forms a part may have been intended as a further piece of semi-mystical writing along the lines of *The Story of My Heart*, but rooted more firmly in his impressions of landscape and wildlife and his emotional and spiritual responses to them. He remembers sights, sounds and his own actions from the early years among the north Wiltshire downs, with the sense that 'they had communicated to me this silent mystery . . . of such I still drink, and hope to do so still deeper'. Few of his short pieces give such important glimpses of Jefferies' fluency and precision when describing general landscapes, mood, the particular details of leaf and insect and his yearning to express a sense of the numinous and the mystical, which he realises may in the end defy verbal expression.

Nature and Books is another piece in which Jefferies considers mankind and its attempts to come to grips with the reality of the natural world, in terms of both its physical reality and the subtle power of its spiritual significance. Its first publication dates from May 1887, just three months before his death, and it reveals a mind at work on the recurrent problem of the inadequacy of words to give an accurate account of the natural world. It begins with a question that combines simplicity and bluntness — 'What is the colour of a dandelion?' — and proceeds to demonstrate that the facile similes and comparisons that come readily to mind simply will not do – 'It is not yellow, nor orange, nor gold; put a sovereign on it and see the difference.' He maintains that we are too ready to use these words in an effort to capture the elusive essence of natural colours, when a moment's reflection would reveal these comparisons to be inaccurate and crass, usually the products of intellectual laziness and a lack of rigour. The challenge is heightened by the shifting quality of the dandelion's colour, which depends upon the quality of the light and the juxtaposition of other colours; for him who struggles to describe it adequately it is like a moving target that is therefore all the more difficult to hit, even with a well-aimed word.

Why do woodland shadows seem bluish? What is the colour of a tree-trunk silhouetted against a bright sky? What is the true colour of an apple, which can look so different when seen from above and below? 'Often in writing about these things I have felt very earnestly my own incompetence to give the least idea of their brilliancy and many-sided colours.' And so the disciplines and practice of science, painting, optics and natural philosophy became for him failed attempts to harness in words the natural qualities of 'the extreme beauties of Nature'. 'Therefore I had to turn back, throw down my books with a bang, and get me to a bit of fallen timber in the open air to meditate.'

Jefferies' meditations are not dismissive of language but filled with optimism that success may yet come, and that it can be achieved in the English language in particular, on behalf of which he makes large and proud claims with respect to its flexibility, expressiveness, subtlety and vigour. 'I say that a great classic thought is greater to an English mind in English words than in any other form . . .' he opined, with a dismissive tone of authority that was probably not justified by any very profound knowledge of ancient or modern languages. Jefferies rejected the claims of Latin, Greek and German, and there is more than a hint of xenophobia in his contempt for French, perhaps a legacy of his unhappy youthful experiences when he briefly ran away from home to travel in France. But he sees no barriers to the power of language eventually finding adequate expression for feelings that are, as yet, inexpressible, and he postulates a theory of language that modern linguistic philosophers might find challenging: because the feelings exist, there must be words to express them.

'How many have said of the sea, "It makes me feel something I cannot say"!

Hence it is clear there exists in the intellect a layer, if I may so call it, of thought yet dumb — chambers within the mind which require the key of new words to unlock.'

So, as yet, all the conventional wisdom and learning of civilisation have failed to describe what is immediately apparent, most powerful and most desirable in Nature – 'There is nothing in books that touches my dandelion.' Even the systematic scientific processes of botanical identification, description and classification have barely touched upon anything more than the margins of understanding. Carl von Linné, the great 'Linnaeus', praised for his industry and hailed for pioneering the close examination of plants, was ultimately relegated to history's lower divisions – 'But no-one reads Linnaeus now . . .' – yet Jefferies aligns himself with the Linnean spirit of inquiry and intimate observation, especially when it is conducted in direct contact with natural things, not in the cloistered seclusion of an herbarium or a laboratory. It is so characteristic of Jefferies that he should have taken most pleasure from Linnaeus' least scientific book, *Tour In Lapland*, an informal account of Scandinavian society that is full of the diversity of human activity in interactive harmony with a magical landscape of unsullied natural surroundings. For Jefferies no landscape was convincing or complete without its people, an opinion which led him to criticise even so well-established a classic as Gilbert White's *Natural History of Selborne* on the grounds that White's countryside lacked human activity: 'It must ever be regretted that he did not leave a natural history of the people of his day . . . a wonderful difference it would have shown.'

In his opinions of Linnaeus and his books, of the writings of the English herbalists Culpeper and Gerard, and of the countless other scholars who spent lifetimes compiling infinitely complex treatises on the phenomena of the natural world, Jefferies is ambivalent. He enjoyed books, both for their contents and as physical artefacts, and the joy of the bibliophile is clear in many of his writings. He speaks feelingly and from experience of the toil involved in preparing, refining, checking and proof-reading a text for the press, yet looks with wonder and a kind of pity on the paltriness of the ultimate achievement of all this effort: 'Boundless is the wealth of Flora's lap; the ingenuity of man has been weaving wreaths out of it for ages, and still the bottom of the sack is not yet . . .' Jefferies seeks something much closer to the essence of Nature than is revealed by all these meticulous books: '. . .I want something more: I want the *soul* of the flowers'. He does not dismiss the writings of scholars or the proliferation of the printed word, but sees this as part of a process leading towards a more complete understanding. Books have helped mankind to 'unlearn' the falsehoods and superstitions of the past, and this process of unlearning will advance when man eventually abandons books – 'the chief value of books is to give us something to unlearn' – and reaches further for fuller understanding: ' . . .by and by, having raised ourselves up upon these huge mounds of facts, we shall begin to see greater things; to do so we must look not at the mound underfoot, but at the starry horizon.' It is a ringing and challenging note on which he ends this, one of his most eagerly optimistic essays, and also one of his last.

Just Before Winter was first published in December 1886, eight months before Jefferies' death. In it he paints a rich portrait of the rural landscape of England in mid-October, as winter approaches, full of carefully observed seasonal details of flowers and herbs, ferns and berries, fungi and stray birds' feathers. This, like most of Jefferies' landscapes, is peppered with human figures, groups of settled labourers and farm workers and nomadic gipsies. The two human types stand distinct from each other; the one rooted in the land, with a profound sense of the turning of the seasons and the religious observances of the year, the other wild and wandering, 'primeval man' with no discernible living faith, but independent and displaying its own ancient integrity.

There is more than a touch of the amateur anthropologist about Jefferies in much of what he wrote: the letters to *The Times* on the social conditions of Wiltshire labourers, which first brought him to public prominence in 1872, have sometimes been criticised for the way Jefferies allegedly looked upon the Wiltshire labourer as if he were no more than a mere anthropological specimen. Here he makes an excursion into comparative anthropology as he considers the gipsies' exotic lives and manners; in relation to the Anglo-Saxon labourers, 'a bit out of the distant Orient under our Western oaks', and what he sees and despises as the 'half-breed . . . who have shown no industry, half-gipsies, who do anything but work . . . with all the blackguardism of both races'. Jefferies' respect for the true travelling gipsies is clear, although he does not understand them, or even particularly try to sympathise with them, which is curious when they so clearly display the close affinity with Nature that Jefferies himself shared. They are 'so old, so very, very old . . . acquiescent to fate, like the red deer', and the forest and heathland is their habitat as they pass through each autumn. But in time some had settled on marginal land, occupying as squatters what was regarded as of no agricultural value, and introducing what Jefferies calls 'the gipsy taint' into the community. He moves from anthropology to amateur eugenics, and finally to sociology in his consideration of the gipsy as a fixed racial type, like the Jews after the Diaspora, and perhaps owing 'that apparent fixidity to their power of mingling with other nations. They are kept alive as races by mixing . . .'

The Water-Colley is a delightful cameo of a wild creature observed in its habitat, the dipper that haunts rocky freshwater streams. This piece of writing first appeared in August 1883 in the *Manchester Guardian* whose editor, C.P. Scott, may have been instrumental in getting Jefferies to visit Somerset in 1882 and again in 1883, when he stayed at Exford in the heart of the stag hunting country, befriended the Heal family of professional hunt servants and gathered material for his book *Red Deer*, which was published in 1883. A week before *The Water-Colley* appeared, Scott had published another short piece by Jefferies on West Country wildlife, entitled *The Otter in Somerset*.

Jefferies gives the dipper its regional West Country name, which is derived from the coal-black of its body colour, and it seems likely that this was his first and perhaps his only encounter with the bird, which was certainly alien to the chalk streams of his native Wiltshire and his adopted Surrey and Sussex, and most common on the hill streams of the West Country, Wales, northern England and Scotland. He went trout fishing in Somerset, and there encountered the bubbling rocky streams that tumble down from the granite uplands of Exmoor, very different in character from the silent power of the spring-fed rivers of the chalk country. *The Water-Colley* stems from observations made on a day's trouting, probably in late May and possibly on the River Barle. As was his habit, Jefferies was readily distracted from thoughts of sport by a desire simply to watch and listen to what was going on around him: even before he gets to the riverside he has been listening to the cuckoo and the corncrake, and has stopped to bend and examine the early purple orchises; and in any case, as he tells us, the still conditions, with low water and bright sunlight, were unpropitious for fly-fishing – 'it is the birds and other creatures peculiar to the water that render fly-fishing so pleasant; were they all destroyed, and nothing left than the mere fish, one might as well stand and fish in a stone cattle-trough'. That 'mere fish' reveals the importance to him of diversity and variety in the natural scene, what Gerard Manley Hopkins described as Nature 'all in a rush with richness'. Jefferies would have approved of the motto of the Fly-fishers Club (*Piscator non solum piscatur* — 'there is more to fishing than catching fish'). He clearly delights in the dipper and its behaviour, and in the river's surroundings, he loves both the wider ambience and the minute details of sight, sound, scent and touch. His scrutiny of the dipper's plumage and coloration is meticulous, and his account of its flight, its crisp calls, its bobbing stance and its busy feeding behaviour has all the close intimacy and accuracy of something seen through binoculars, bright and clear, and heard at close quarters. In this, as in so much of his writing, he reveals his gifts as a field naturalist, with an alert eye for minute details and always a questioning desire to know 'how?' and 'why?' He ends this essay with a simple plea, that this alleged but unlikely predator of trout eggs and fry should be spared unthinking persecution by 'lovers of sport', and urges that the water-colley should be respected and preserved, by them as by him, as the sprightly *genius loci* of these tumbling western rivers.

In this selection, Jefferies' most sustained and intimate piece of observation of a single wild creature comes in *The Rookery*, which was first published in the *Pall Mall Gazette* in 1878 and later used as a chapter in one of his most popular book-length accounts of the natural scene, *Wild Life in a Southern County*. It is characteristic of Jefferies that he should have chosen to focus so closely on such a common and familiar bird of English farmland and woodlands. He was able to find endless absorbing interest in so many things which for most other people had lost their freshness and appeal simply because they were so ubiquitous. This account of rooks through the year is closely observed and detailed, the outcome of many hours and days of the careful watching at which Jefferies was so uniquely skilful. He had a disciplined and analytical eye for the smallest details, and this becomes immediately apparent from the outset in his meticulous descriptions of where and how the rooks go about constructing their nests. Few writers before or since have devoted such obvious care to a consideration of how one common species of bird locates and builds its nests, and Jefferies' third paragraph is an outstanding piece of detailed yet economical description of the six principal criteria which he observed as essential for the successful positioning and building of the nests. Only a careful eye applied to rookeries over successive seasons could have noticed how the birds seem able to detect when a nesting elm is dying and abandon it before the signs of incipient decay have become apparent to any but the most careful human observer.

As always, the landscape in which Jefferies' wild creatures roam is a well-peopled one, seldom lacking bustling human activity. For landowners and their guests and the local country people there is the annual ritual of shooting the young fledgling rooks in May, for sport and for the kitchen. There is ample evidence that Jefferies is writing from direct and probably repeated experience, for who but a practitioner would know that young rooks' feathers are so soft as to make them easy victims to a long shot, or that the young birds are verminous and need careful handling when the young boys go about collecting those that have been shot? The annual shooting of rooks in May was a common enough activity in late Victorian England, which is perhaps why Jefferies spends comparatively little time describing it, though what he relates is intensely vivid, accurate, without illusions and wholly devoid of the mawkish sentimentality that might have marred many such accounts by contemporary writers. But much less familiar is the roguery of robbing a rookery, an altogether more furtive affair in which the local lads, especially the more nimble and daring, would scale the high nesting trees to take the young branchers alive — a worthwhile exercise in gathering food for tenants and cottagers who appreciated a rook pie on the table, with the added spice of danger for the climbers and the general sense of satisfaction at outwitting landowners and shooting tenants, perhaps on the very eve of their carefully planned shooting parties. Jefferies concludes with a description of the steady and methodical feeding of the rooks in autumn and winter, their typically corvine wariness of guns and brandished sticks, and their distinctive styles of flight under different circumstances in comparison with those of the more solitary carrion crow — all small and telling details that testify to the carefulness of the writer's repeated observations of these common yet absorbing and often overlooked birds.

The Acorn-Gatherer, first published in March 1883 in *Longman's Magazine*, is rather unusual in manner and tone for Jefferies, and it can be invoked as a powerful antidote to any temptation to view him merely as a writer of comfortable rural idylls. In its economically stark depiction of individual human suffering and eventual tragedy it is as bleak and desolate as anything by Thomas Hardy. The boy's fate is magnified in its hopelessness by the indifference of the cattle dealer, the barge woman and the labourer, who each turn away from the event, absorbed in their own affairs. About suffering he was never wrong, like the 'Old Masters' in Auden's *Musée des Beaux Arts*; and although he may have lacked the novelist's essential skills of detailed and evolving characterisation, Jefferies nevertheless succeeds in creating an arresting and wholly convincing interaction of characters for this tragic cameo.

An English Deer Park is an essay in the best style of Jefferies' mature years, although it was not published until a year after his death, appearing in *Century Illustrated Monthly Magazine* in October 1888. It combines important elements of Jefferies' sense of rural history and continuity with the detailed and restrainedly lyrical descriptions of a much-loved landscape, and is set within the confines of a well-established park on a landed estate, largely seen through the eyes and mirrored in the behaviour of the estate's oldest and most influential tenant, the land steward, whom the other tenants defer to by the name of 'the squire'. From his gun-room window in the old manor house — now abandoned by the landowner for a new mansion closer to the village — he looks out on familiar acres of grassland and woods that are something of a microcosm of rural England though sheltered from it behind the old and moss-grown walls of the park, sequestered and lush in contrast with the dry dust of the roads and the baking heat of the open cornfields. Here Jefferies finds himself in an ambience where both landscape and wildlife hint at the historical continuum he prizes – 'a little piece of olden England without its terror and bloodshed' – , where enclosed deer still wander as reminders of the hunted wild deer of old, the victims of furious pursuits and the early weapons of arrow, longbow and crossbow. The squire and the modern foresters are the heirs of that long hunting tradition, although theirs are the double-barrelled guns and rifles of modern technology; yet the old ways are not entirely intact, for so much of the immemorially ancient deer lore and the archaic terms of venery had been lost. (Somerset, where Jefferies studied the wild deer and the continuing traditions of stag hunting with hounds, came as a delightful revelation to him when he went there in 1882-83, gathering materials for his book *Red Deer* that appeared in the latter year.) Yet the deer themselves are, by their mere presence, tangible living reminders of the rural heritage of old England, just as the natural landscape of the park represents for Jefferies an pleasureable and wholly appropriate environment untouched by the attentions of landscape gardeners of 'that artificial era', when their interventions 'to make the engraver's ideal landscape of straight vistas' had produced so many 'hideous disfigurements of beautiful scenery'. He concludes with the emphatic assertion that 'our English landscape wants no gardening: it *cannot* be gardened. The least interference kills it.' It is a statement that was to be echoed a generation later by Hopkins, when he wrote in *Binsey Poplars*:

> 'O, if we but knew what we do
> When we delve and hew,
> Hack and wrack the growing green . . .
> After-comers cannot guess the beauty been . . .
> Her being so tender . . .
> That even when we seek to mend her
> We end her.'

This is one of the comparatively rare occasions when Jefferies implies that only man and his works are vile in a landscape where every natural prospect pleases him so much.

And yet the elderly squire is an essential component in the enduring landscape, as natural as the deer and the trees and the grassland, and like Jefferies himself he is an observer and commentator on the scene as he surveys it from his gun-room window or walks about it with a favourite gun underneath his arm. 'Without a gun the woods lost half their meaning for him' Jefferies writes, and elsewhere describes how he, too, often went out into the fields and woods of his native Wiltshire and his adopted Surrey and Sussex with a gun tucked under his arm: 'I used to take a gun for nominal occupation, and sit in the hedge for hours . . . In the end the gun remained unused . . . Destruction in itself was not the motive; it was an overpowering instinct for woods and fields . . . Watching so often stayed the shot that at last it grew to be a habit.' In much of his writing Richard Jefferies takes for granted what many modern commentators would question or seem unaware of, that hunting is a natural, deep-rooted and atavistic impulse in man, and that the formalised field sports of a settled and developed civilisation are the contemporary expression of this. The stealthy and careful observation of wild creatures, too, is for Jefferies a sublimation of the same rooted hunting impulses, which for him involved going equipped to shoot but instead 'staying the shot' in rapt attention at what he saw and heard.

Field Sports in Art, which was first printed in the *Art Journal* in April 1885, looks at hunting and shooting from the perspective of the participants' recollection and celebration of the chase and the quarry, an impulse that links early man and contemporary Victorian sportsmen in a common desire to immortalise their hunting in enduring images, whether it be carvings and paintings on the walls of caves or engravings on the lock-plates of modern sporting guns. (Ironically, the engraving of gun-locks which Jefferies urges has always remained an uncommon and largely alien tradition in British gunmaking, though widespread and much admired in European and American work.) Jefferies sees dreams as the personal and subjective forms in which hunting achieves a kind of immortality and mythic status, of which painted and engraved images are the natural external expression. Early civilisations saw the stellar constellations in terms of Orion, the huntsman, and other representations of the chase which was not merely a practical means of food-gathering or an exciting sporting diversion but also a ritual of profound and continuing significance in expressing mankind's relationship with the natural world.

In all the pieces collected in the present anthology, Richard Jefferies explores and expounds important aspects of his philosophy of the inter-relationship of humanity and the natural scene. The common theme is invariably a feeling of delighted and enriched involvement, of the deepening and fulfilling sense of wonder that stems from the writer's profound attachment to his beloved land and the human figures that people it. The continuing interest in his writings, many of which have remained in print and been readily available throughout the century and more since his death, is persuasive evidence of the special skill with which he struck a responsive chord in his sensitive essays on the English landscape, its wild creatures and its people.

Colin McKelvie
Dumfriesshire
June 1994

Meadow Thoughts

THE OLD house stood by the silent country road, secluded by many a long, long mile, and yet again secluded within the great walls of the garden. Often and often I rambled up to the milestone which stood under an oak, to look at the chipped inscription low down — 'To London, 79 miles.' So far away, you see, that the very inscription was cut at the foot of the stone, since no-one would be likely to want that information. It was half hidden by docks and nettles, despised and unnoticed. A broad land this seventy-nine miles — how many meadows and cornfields, hedges and woods, in that distance? — wide enough to seclude any house, to hide it like an acorn in the grass. Those who have lived all their lives in remote places do not feel the remoteness. No one else seemed to be conscious of the breadth that separated the place from the great centre, but it was, perhaps, that consciousness which deepened the solitude to me. It made the silence more still; the shadows of the oaks yet slower in their movement, everything in earnest. To convey a full impression of the intense concentration of Nature in the meadows is very difficult — everything is so utterly oblivious of man's thought and man's heart. The oaks stand — quiet, still — so still that the lichen loves them. At their feet the grass grows, and heeds nothing. Among it the squirrels leap, and their little hearts are as far away from you or me as the very wood of the oaks. The sunshine settles itself in the valley by the brook, and abides there whether we come or not. Glance through the gap in the hedge by the oak, and see how concentrated it is — all of it, every blade of grass, and leaf, and flower, and living creature, finch or squirrel. It is mesmerised upon itself. Then I used to feel that it really was seventy-nine miles to London, and not an hour or two only by rail, really all those miles. A great, broad province of green furrow and ploughed furrow between the old house and the city of the world. Such solace and solitude seventy-nine miles thick cannot be painted; the trees cannot be placed far enough away in perspective. It is necessary to stay in it like the oaks to know it.

Lime tree branches overhung the corner of the garden wall, whence a view was easy of the silent and dusty road, till over-arching oaks concealed it. The white dust heated by the sunshine, the green hedges, and the heavily massed trees, white clouds rolled together in the sky, a footpath opposite lost in the fields, as you might thrust a stick into the grass, tender lime leaves caressing the cheek, and silence. That is, the silence of the fields. If a breeze rustled the boughs, if a greenfinch called, if the cart-mare in the meadow shook herself, making the earth and air tremble by her with the convulsion of her mightly muscles, these were not sounds, they were the silence itself. So sensitive to it as I was, in its turn it held me firmly, like the fabled spells of old time. The mere touch of a leaf was a talisman to bring me under the enchantment, so that I seemed to feel and know all that was proceeding among the grass-blades and in the bushes. Among the lime trees along the wall the birds never built, though so close and sheltered. They built everywhere but there. To the broad coping-stones of the wall under the lime boughs speckled thrushes came almost hourly, sometimes to peer out and reconnoitre if it was safe to visit the garden, sometimes to see if a snail had climbed up the ivy. Then they dropped quietly down into the long strawberry patch immediately under. The cover of strawberries is the constant resource of all creeping things; the thrushes looked round every plant and under every leaf and runner. One toad always resided there, often two, and as you gathered a ripe strawberry you might catch sight of his black eye watching you take the fruit he had saved for you.

Down the road skims an eave-swallow, swift as an arrow, his white back making the sun-dried dust dull and dingy; he is seeking a pool for mortar, and will waver to and fro by the brook below till he finds a convenient place to alight. Thence back to the eave here, where for forty years he and his ancestors built in safety. Two white butterflies fluttering round each other rise over the limes, once more up over the house, and soar on till their white shows no longer against the illuminated air. A grasshopper calls on the sward by the strawberries, and immediately fillips himself over seven leagues of grass blades. Yonder a line of men and women file across the field, seen for a moment as they pass a gateway, and the hay changes from hay-colour to green behind them as they turn the under but still sappy side upwards. They are working hard, but it looks easy, slow, and sunny. Finches fly out from the hedgerow to the overturned hay. Another butterfly, a brown one, floats along the dusty road — the only traveller yet. The white clouds are slowly passing behind the oaks, large puffed clouds, like deliberate loads of hay, leaving little wisps and flecks behind them caught in the sky. How pleasant it would be to read in the shadow! There is a broad shadow on the sward by the strawberries cast by a tall and fine-grown American crab tree. The very place for a book; and although I know it is useless, yet I go and fetch one and dispose myself on the grass.

I can never read in summer out of doors. Though in shadow the bright light fills it, summer shadows are broadest daylight. The page is so white and hard, the letters so very black, the meaning and drift not quite intelligible, because neither eye nor mind will dwell upon it. Human thoughts and imaginings written down are pale and feeble in bright

summer light. The eye wanders away, and rests more lovingly on greensward and green lime leaves. The mind wanders yet deeper and farther into the dreamy mystery of the azure sky. Once now and then, determined to write down that mystery and delicious sense while actually in it, I have brought out table and ink and paper, and sat there in the midst of the summer day. Three words, and where is the thought? Gone. The paper is so obviously paper, the ink so evidently ink, the pen so stiff; all so inadequate. You want colour, flexibility, light, sweet low sound — all these to paint it and play it in music, at the same time you want something that will answer to and record in one touch the strong throb of life and the thought and feeling, or whatever it is that goes out into the earth and sky and space, endless as a beam of light. The very shade of the pen on the paper tells you how utterly hopeless it is to express these things. There is the shade and the brilliant gleaming whiteness; now tell me in plain written words the simple contrast of the two. Not in twenty pages, for the bright light shows the paper in its common fibre-ground, coarse aspect, in its reality, not as a mind-tablet.

The delicacy and beauty of thought or feeling is so extreme that it cannot be inked in; it is like the green and blue of field and sky, of veronica flower and grass blade, which in their own existence throw light and beauty on each other, but in artificial colours repel. Take the table indoors again, and the book; the thoughts and imaginings of others are vain, and of your own too deep to be written. For the mind is filled with the exceeding beauty of these things, and their great wondrousness and marvel. Never yet have I been able to write what I felt about the sunlight only. Colour and form and light are as magic to me. It is a trance. It requires a language of ideas to convey it. It is ten years since I last reclined on that grass plot, and yet I have been writing of it as if it was yesterday, and every blade of grass is as visible and as real to me now as then. They were greener towards the house, and more brown-tinted on the margin of the strawberry bed, because towards the house the shadow rested longest. By the strawberries the fierce sunlight burned them.

The sunlight put out the books I brought into it just as it put out the fire on the hearth indoors. The tawny flames floating upwards could not bite the crackling sticks when the full beams came pouring on them. Such extravagance of light overcame the little fire till it was screened from the power of the heavens. So here in the shadow of the American crab tree the light of the sky put out the written pages. For this beautiful and wonderful light excited a sense of some likewise beautiful and wonderful truth, some unknown but grand thought hovering as a swallow above. The swallows hovered and did not alight, but they were there. An inexpressible thought quivered in the azure overhead; it could not be fully grasped, but there was a sense and feeling of its presence. Before that mere sense of its presence the weak and feeble pages, the small fires of human knowledge, dwindled and lost meaning. There was something here that was not in the books. In all the philosophies and searches of mind there was nothing that could be brought to face it, to say 'this is what it intends, this is the explanation of the dream.' The very grass-blades confounded the wisest, the tender lime leaf put them to shame, the grasshopper derided them, the sparrow on the wall chirped his scorn. The books were put out, unless a screen were placed between them and the light of the sky — that is, an assumption, so as to make an artificial mental darkness. Grant some assumptions — that is, screen off the light — and in that darkness everything was easily arranged, this thing here and that yonder. But Nature grants no assumptions, and the books were put out. There is something beyond the philosophies in the light, in the grass-blades, the leaf, the grasshopper, the sparrow on the wall. Some day the great and beautiful thought which hovers on the confines of the mind will at last alight. In that is hope, the whole sky is full of abounding hope. Something beyond the books, that is consolation.

The little lawn beside the strawberry bed, burned brown there, and green towards the house shadow, holds how many myriad grass-blades? Here they are all matted together, long and dragging each other down. Part them, and beneath them are still more, overhung and hidden. The fibres are intertangled, woven in an endless basketwork and chaos of green and dried threads. A blameable profusion this; a fifth as many would be enough; altogether a wilful waste here. As for these insects that spring out of it as I press the grass, a hundredth part of them would suffice. The American crab tree is a snowy mount in spring; the flakes of bloom, when they fall, cover the grass with a film — a bushel of bloom, which the wind takes and scatters afar. The extravagance is sublime. The two little cherry trees are so wasteful; they throw away handfuls of flower: but in the meadows the careless, spendthrift ways of grass and flower and all things are not to be expressed. Seeds by the hundred million float with absolute indifference on the air. The oak has a hundred thousand more leaves than necessary, and never hides a single acorn. Nothing utilitarian — everything on a scale of splendid waste. Such noble, broadcast, open-armed waste is delicious to behold. Never was there such a lying proverb as 'Enough is as good as a feast'. Give me the feast; give me squandered millions of seeds, luxurious carpets of petals, green mountains of oak leaves. The greater the waste, the greater the enjoyment — the nearer the approach to real life. Casuistry is of no avail; the fact is obvious; Nature flings treasures abroad, puffs them with open lips along on every breeze, piles up lavish layers of them in the free open air, packs countless numbers together in the needles of a fir tree. Prodigality and superfluity are stamped on everything she does. The ear of wheat returns a hundredfold the grain from which it grew. The surface of the earth offers to us far more than we can consume — the grains, the seeds, the fruits, the animals, the abounding products are beyond the power of all the human race to devour. They can, too, be multiplied a thousandfold. There is no natural lack. Whenever there is lack among us it is from artificial causes, which intelligence should remove.

From the littleness, and meanness, and niggardliness forced upon us by circumstances, what a relief to turn aside to the exceeding plenty of Nature! There are no bounds to it, there is no comparison to parallel it, so great is this generosity. No physical reason exists why every human being should not have sufficient, at least, of necessities. For any human being to starve, or even to be in trouble about the procuring of simple food, appears, indeed, a strange and unaccountable thing, quite upside down, and contrary to sense, if you do but consider a moment the enormous profusion the earth throws at our feet. In the slow process of time, as the human heart grows larger, such provision, I sincerely trust, will be made that no one need ever feel anxiety about mere subsistence. Then, too, let there be some imitation of this open-handed generosity and divine waste. Let the generations to come feast free of care, like my finches on the seeds of the mowing-grass, from which no voice drives them. If I could but give away as freely as the earth does!

The white-backed eave-swallow has returned many, many times from the shallow drinking-place by the brook to his half-built nest. Sometimes the pair of them cling to the mortar they have fixed under the eave, and twitter to each other about the progress of the work. They dive downwards with such velocity when they quit hold that it seems as if they must strike the ground, but they shoot up again, over the wall and the lime trees. A thrush has been to the arbour yonder twenty times; it is made of crossed laths, and overgrown with 'tea-plant', and the nest is inside the lath-work. A sparrow has visited the rose tree by the wall — the buds are covered with aphids. A brown tree-creeper has been to the limes, then to the cherries, and even to a stout lilac stem. No matter how small the tree, he tries all that are in his way. The bright colours of a bullfinch were visible a moment just now, as he passed across the

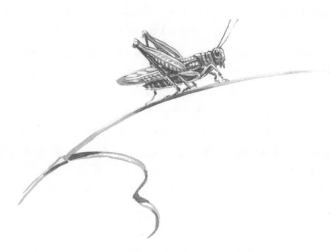

shadows farther down the garden under the damson trees and into the bushes. The grasshopper has gone past and along the garden path, his voice is not heard now; but there is another coming. While I have been dreaming, all these and hundreds out in the meadow have been intensely happy. So concentrated on their little work in the sunshine, so intent on the tiny egg, on the insect captured, on the grass-tip to be carried to the eager fledglings, so joyful in listening to the song poured out for them or in pouring it forth, quite oblivious of all else. It is in the intense concentration that they are so happy. If they could only live longer! — but a few such seasons for them — I wish they could live a hundred years just to feast on the seeds and sing and be utterly happy and oblivious to everything but the moment they are passing. A black line has rushed up from the espalier apple yonder to the housetop thirty times at least. The starlings fly so swiftly and so straight that they seem to leave a black line along the air. They have a nest in the roof, they are to and fro it and the meadow the entire day, from dawn till eve. The espalier apple, like a screen, hides the meadow from me, so that the descending starlings appear to dive into a space behind it. Sloping downwards the meadow makes a valley; I cannot see it, but know that it is golden with buttercups, and that a brook runs in the groove of it.

Afar yonder I can see a summit beyond which the swells upwards to a higher level than this spot. There are bushes and elms whose height is decreased by distance on the summit, horses in the shadow of the trees, and a small flock of sheep crowded, as is their wont, in the hot and sunny gateway. By the side of the summit is a deep green trench, so it looks from here, in the hillside: it is really the course of a streamlet worn deep in the earth. I can see nothing between the top of the espalier screen and the horses under the elms on the hill. But the starlings go up and down into the hollow space, which is aglow with golden buttercups, and, indeed, I am looking over a hundred finches eagerly searching, sweetly calling, happy as the summer day. A thousand thousand grasshoppers are leaping, thrushes are labouring, filled with love and tenderness, doves cooing — there is as much joy as there are leaves on the hedges. Faster than the starling's flight my mind runs up to the streamlet in the deep green trench beside the hill.

Pleasant it was to trace it upwards, narrowing at every ascending step, till the thin stream, thinner than fragile glass, did but merely slip over the stones. A little less and it could not have run at all, water could not stretch out to greater tenuity. It smoothed the brown growth on the stones, stroking it softly. It filled up tiny basins of sand and ran out at the edges between minute rocks of flint. Beneath it went under thickest brooklime, blue-flowered, and serrated water-parsnips, lost like many a mighty river for a while among a forest of leaves. Higher up masses of bramble and projecting thorn stopped the explorer, who must wind round the grassy mound. Pausing to look back a moment there were meads under the hill with the shortest and greenest herbage, perpetually watered, and without one single buttercup, a strip of pure green among yellow flowers and yellowing corn. A few hollow oaks on whose boughs the cuckoos stayed to call, two or three peewits coursing up and down, larks singing, and for all else silence. Between the wheat and the grassy mound the path was almost closed, burdocks and brambles thrust the adventurer outwards to brush against the wheatears. Upwards till suddenly it turned, and led by steep notches in the bank, as it seemed, down to the roots of the elm trees. The clump of elms grew right over a deep and rugged hollow; their branches reached out across it, roofing in the cave.

Here was the spring, at the foot of a perpendicular rock, moss-grown low down, and overrun with creeping ivy higher. Green thorn bushes filled the chinks and made a wall to the well, and the long narrow hart's-tongue streaked the face of the cliff. Behind the thick thorns hid the course of the streamlet, in front rose the solid rock, upon the right hand the sward came to the edge — it shook every now and then as the horses in the shade of the elms stamped their feet — on the left hand the ears of wheat peered over the verge. A rocky cell in concentrated silence of green things. Now and again a finch, a starling or a sparrow would come meaning to drink — athirst from the meadow or the cornfield — and start and almost entangle their wings in the bushes, so completely astonished that anyone should be there. The spring rises in a hollow under the rock imperceptibly, and without bubble or sound. The fine sand of the shallow basin is undisturbed — no tiny water-volcano pushes up a dome of particles. Nor is there any crevice in the stone, but the basin is always full and always running over. As it slips from the brim a gleam of sunshine falls through the boughs and meets it. To this cell I used to come once now and then on a summer's day, tempted, perhaps, like the finches, by the sweet cool water, but drawn also by a feeling that could not be analysed. Stooping, I lifted the water in the hollow of my hand — carefully, lest the sand might be disturbed — and the sunlight gleamed on it as it slipped through my fingers. Alone in the green-roofed cave, alone with the sunlight and the pure water, there was a sense of something more than these. The water was more to me than water, and the sun than sun. The gleaming rays on the water in my palm held me for a moment, the touch of the water gave me something from itself. A moment, and the gleam was gone, the water flowing away, but I had had them. Beside the physical water and physical light I had received from them their beauty; they had communicated to me this silent mystery. The pure and beautiful water, the pure, clear and beautiful light, each had given me something of their truth.

So many times I came to it, toiling up the long and shadowless hill in the burning sunshine, often carrying a vessel to take some of it home with me. There was a brook, indeed; but this was different, it was the spring; it was taken home as a beautiful flower might be brought. It is not the physical water, it is the sense of feeling that it conveys. Nor is it the physical sunshine; it is the sense of inexpressible beauty which it brings with it. Of such I still drink, and hope to do so still deeper.

The Life of the Fields, 5 April 1884

Nature and Books

WHAT IS the colour of the dandelion? There are many dandelions: that which I mean flowers in May, when the meadow-grass has started and the hares are busy by daylight. That which flowers very early in the year has a thickness of hue, and is not interesting; in autumn the dandelions quite change their colour and are pale. The right dandelion for this question is the one that comes about May with a very broad disc, and in such quantities as often to cover a whole meadow. I used to admire them very much in the fields by Surbiton (strong clay soil), and also on the towing-path of the Thames where the sward is very broad, opposite Long Ditton; indeed, I have often walked up that towing-path on a beautiful sunny morning, when all was quiet except the nightingales in the Palace hedge, on purpose to admire them. I dare say they are all gone now for evermore; still, it is a pleasure to look back on anything beautiful. What colour is this dandelion? It is not yellow, nor orange, nor gold; put a sovereign on it and see the difference. They say the gipsies call it the Queen's great hairy dog-flower — a number of words to one stalk; and so, to get a colour to it, you may call it the yellow-gold-orange plant. In the winter, on the black mud under a dark, dripping tree, I found a piece of orange peel, lately dropped — a bright red orange speck in the middle of the blackness. It looked very beautiful, and instantly recalled to my mind the great dandelion discs in the sunshine of summer. Yet certainly they are not red-orange. Perhaps, if ten people answered this question, they would

each give different answers. Again, a bright day or a cloudy, the presence of a slight haze, or the juxtaposition of other colours, alters it very much; for the dandelion is not a glazed colour, like the buttercup, but sensitive. It is like a sponge, and adds to its own hue that which is passing, sucking it up.

The shadows of the trees in the wood, why are they blue? Ought they not to be dark? Is it really blue, or an illusion? And what is their colour when you see the shadow of a tall trunk aslant in the air like a leaning pillar? The fallen brown leaves wet with dew have a different brown from those that are dry, and the upper surface of the green growing leaf is different from the under surface. The yellow butterfly, if you meet one in October, has so toned down his spring yellow that you might fancy him a pale green leaf floating along the road. There is a shining, quivering, gleaming; there is a changing, fluttering, shifting; there is a mixing, weaving — varnished wings, translucent wings, wings with dots and veins, all playing over the purple heath; a very tangle of many-toned lights and hues. Then come the apples: if you look upon them from an upper window, so as to glance along the level plane of the fruit, delicate streaks of scarlet, like those that lie parallel to the eastern horizon before sunrise; golden tints under bronze, and apple-green, and some that the wasps have hollowed, more glowingly beautiful than the rest; sober leaves and black and white swallows: to see it you must be high up, as if the apples were strewn on a sward of foliage. So have I gone in three steps from May dandelion to September apple; an immense space measured by things beautiful, so filled that ten folio volumes could not hold the description of them, and I have left out the meadows, the brooks, and hills. Often in writing about these things I have felt very earnestly my own incompetence to give the least idea of their brilliancy and many-sided colours. My gamut was so very limited in its terms, and would not give a note to one in a thousand of those I saw. At last I said, I will have more words; I will have more terms; I will have a book on colour, and I will find and use the right technical name for each one of these lovely tints. I was told that the very best book was by Chevreul, which had tinted illustrations, chromatic scales, and all that could be desired.

Quite true, all of it; but for me it contained nothing. There was a good deal about assorted wools, but nothing about leaves; nothing by which I could tell you the difference between the light scarlet of one poppy and the deep purple-scarlet of another species. The dandelion remained unexplained; as for the innumerable other flowers, and wings, and sky-colours, they were not even approached. The book, in short, dealt with the artificial and not with nature. Next I went to science — works on optics, such a mass of them. Some I had read in old time, and turned to again; some I read for the first time, some translated from the German, and so on. It appeared that, experimenting with physical colour, tangible paint, they had found out that red, yellow, and blue were the three primary colours; and then, experimenting with light itself, with colours not tangible, they found out that red, green and violet were the three primary colours; but neither of these would do for the dandelion. Once upon a time I had taken an interest in spectrum analysis, and the theory of the polarization of light was fairly familiar; any number of books, but not what I wanted to know. Next the idea occurred to me of buying all the colours used in painting, and tinting as many pieces of paper a separate hue, and so comparing these with petals, and wings, and grass, and trifolium. This did not answer at all; my unskilful hands made a very poor wash, and the yellow paper set by a yellow petal did not agree, the scientific reason of which I cannot enter into now. Secondly, the names attached to many of these paints are unfamiliar to general readers; it is doubtful if bistre, Leitch's blue, oxide of chromium, and so on, would convey an idea. They might as well be Greek symbols: no use to attempt to describe hues of heath or hill in that way. These, too, are only distinct colours. What was to be done with all the shades and tones? Still there remained the language of the studio; without doubt a master of painting could be found who would quickly supply the technical term of anything I liked to show him; but again no use, because it would be technical. And a still more insurmountable difficulty occurs: in so far as I have looked at pictures, it seems as if the artists had met with the same obstacle in paints as I have in words — that is to say, a deficiency. Either painting is incompetent to express the extreme beauty of nature, or in some way the canons of art forbid the attempt. Therefore I had to turn back, throw down my books with a bang, and get me to a bit of fallen timber in the open air to mediate.

Would it be possible to build up a fresh system of colour language by means of natural objects? Could we say pine-wood green, larch green, spruce green, wasp yellow, bumble-bee amber? And there are fungi that have marked tints, but the Latin names of these agarics are not pleasant. Butterfly blue — but there are several varieties; and this plan is interfered with by two things: first, that almost every single item of nature, however minute, has got a distinctly different colour, so that the dictionary of tints would be immense; and next, so very few would know the object itself that the colour attached to it would have no meaning. The power of language has been gradually enlarging for a great length of time, and I venture to say that the English language at the present time can express more, and is more subtle, flexible, and, at the same time, vigorous, than any of which we possess a record. When people talk to me about studying Sanskrit, or Greek, or Latin, or German, or, still more absurd, French, I feel as if I could fell them with a mallet happily. Study the English, and you will find everything there, I reply. With such a language I fully anticipate, in years to come, a great development in the power of expressing thoughts and feelings which are now thoughts and feelings only. How many have said of the sea, 'It makes me feel something I cannot say'! Hence it is clear there exists in the intellect a layer, if I may so call it, of thought yet dumb — chambers within the mind which require the key of new words to unlock. Whenever that is done a fresh impetus is given to human progress. There are a million books, and yet with all their aid I cannot tell you the colour of the May dandelion. There are three greens at this moment in my mind: that of the leaf of the flower-de-luce, that of the yellow iris leaf, and that of the bayonet-like leaf of the common flag. With admission to a million books, how am I to tell you the difference between these tints? So many, many books, and such a very, very little bit of nature in them! Though we have been so many thousand years upon the earth we do not seem to have done any more as yet than walk along beaten footpaths, and sometimes really it would seem as if there were something in the minds of many men quite artificial, quite distinct from the sun and trees and hills — altogether house people, whose gods must be set in four-cornered buildings. There is nothing in books that touches my dandelion.

It grows, ah yes, it grows! How does it grow? Builds itself up somehow of sugar and starch, and turns mud into bright colour and dead earth into food for bees, and some day perhaps for you, and knows when to shut its petals, and how to construct the brown seeds to float with the wind, and how to please the children, and how to puzzle me. Ingenious dandelion! If you find out that its correct botanical name is *Leontodon taraxacum*, or *Leontodon densleonis*, that will bring it into botany; and there is a place called Dandelion Castle in Kent, and a bell with the inscription —

> John de Dandelion with his great dog
> Brought over this bell on a mill cog —

which is about as relevant as the mere words *Leontodon taraxacum*. Botany is the knowledge of plants according to the accepted definition; naturally, therefore, when I began to think I would like to know a little more of flowers than could be learned by seeing them in the fields, I went to botany. Nothing could be more simple. You buy a book which first of all tells you how to recognize them, how to classify them; next instructs you in their uses, medical or economical; next tells you about the folklore and curious associations; next enters into a lucid explanation of the physiology of the plant and its relation to other creatures; and finally, and most important, supplies you with the ethical feeling, the ideal aspiration to be identified with each particular flower. One moderately thick volume would probably suffice for such a modest round as this.

Lo! now the labour of Hercules when he set about bringing up Cerberus from below, and all the work done by Apollo in the years when he ground corn, are but a little matter compared with the attempt to master botany. Great minds have been at it these two thousand years, and yet we are still only nibbling at the edge of the leaf, as the ploughboys bite the young hawthorn in spring. The mere classification — all plant-lore was a vast chaos till there came the man of Sweden, the great Linnaeus, till the sexes were recognized, and everything was ruled out and set in place again. A wonderful man! I think it would be true to say it was Linnaeus who set the world on its present twist of thinking, and levered our mental glove a little more perpendicular to the ecliptic. He actually gathered the dandelion and took it to bits like a scientific child; he touched nature with his fingers instead of sitting looking out of the window — perhaps the first man who had ever done so for seventeen hundred years or so, since superstition blighted the progress of pagan Rome. The work he did! But no one reads Linnaeus now, the folios, indeed, might moulder to dust without loss, because his spirit has got into the minds of men, and the text is of little consequence. The best book he wrote to read now is the delightful *Tour in Lapland*, with its quaint pen-and-ink sketches, so realistically vivid, as if the thing sketched had been banged on the paper and so left its impress. I have read it three times, and I still cherish the old yellow pages; it is the best botanical book, written by the greatest of botanists, specially sent on a botanical expedition, and it contains nothing about botany. It tells you about the canoes, and the hard cheese, and the Laplander's warehouse on top of a pole, like a pigeon-house; and the innocent way in which the maiden helped the traveller in his bath, and how the aged men ran so fast that the devil could not catch them; and, best of all, because it gives a smack in the face to modern pseudo-scientific medical cant about hygiene, showing how the Laplanders break every 'law', human and 'divine', ventilation, bath and diet — all the trash — and therefore enjoy the most excellent health, and live to a great old age. Still I have not succeeded in describing the immense labour there was in learning to distinguish plants on the Linnaean system. Then comes in order of time the natural system, the geographical distribution; then there is the geological relationship, so to say, to Pliocene plants, natural selection and evolution. Of that let us say nothing; let sleeping dogs lie, and evolution is a very weary dog. Most charming, however, will be found the later studies of naturalists on the interdependence of flowers and insects; there is another work the dandelion has got to do — endless, endless botany! Where did the plants come from at first? Did they come creeping up out of the sea at the edge of the estuaries, and gradually run their roots into the ground, and so make green the earth? Did Man come out of the sea, as the Greeks thought? There are so many ideas in plants. Flora, with a full lap, scattering knowledge and flowers together; everything good and sweet seems to come out of flowers, up to the very highest thoughts of the soul, and we carry them daily to the very threshold of the other world. Next you may try the microscope and its literature, and find the crystals in the rhubarb.

I remember taking sly glances when I was a very little boy at an old Culpeper's *Herbal*, heavily bound in leather and curiously illustrated. It was so deliciously wicked to read about the poisons; and I thought perhaps it was a book like that, only in papyrus rolls, that was used by the sorceress who got ready the poisoned mushrooms in old Rome. Youth's ideas are so imaginative, and bring together things that are so widely separated. Conscience told me I had no business to read about poisons; but there was a fearful fascination in hemlock, and I recollect tasting a little bit — it was very nasty. At this day, nevertheless, if any one wishes to begin a pleasant, interesting, unscientific acquaintance with

English plants, he would do very well indeed to get a good copy of Culpeper. Grey hairs had insisted on showing themselves in my beard when, all those weary years afterwards, I thought I would like to buy the still older Englishman, Gerard, who had no Linnaeus to guide him, who walked about our English lanes centuries ago. What wonderful scenes he must have viewed when they were all a tangle of wild flowers, and plants that are now scarce were common, and the old ploughs, and the curious customs, and the wild red-deer — it would make a good picture, it really would, Gerard studying English orchids! Such a volume! — hundreds of pages, yellow of course, close type, and marvellously well printed. The minute care they must have taken in those early days of printing to get up such a book — a wonderful volume both in bodily shape and contents. Just then the only copy I could hear of was much damaged. The cunning old bookseller said he could make it up; but I have no fancy for patched books, they are not genuine; I would rather have them deficient; and the price was rather long, and so I went Gerardless. Of folklore and medicinal use and history and associations here you have hints. The bottom of the sack is not yet; there are the monographs, years of study expended upon one species of plant growing in one locality, perhaps; some made up into thick books and some into broad quarto pamphlets, with most beautiful plates, that, if you were to see them, would tempt you to cut them out and steal them, all sunk and lost like dead ships under the sand: piles of monographs. There are warehouses in London that are choked to the beams of the roof with them, and every fresh exploration furnishes another shelf-load. The source of the Nile was unknown a very few years ago, and now, I have no doubt, there are dozens of monographs on the flowers that flourish there. Indeed, there is not a thing that grows that may not furnish a monograph. The author spends perhaps twenty years in collecting his material, during which time he must of course come across a great variety of amusing information, and then he spends another ten years writing out a fair copy of his labours. Then he thinks it does not quite do in that form, so he snips a paragraph out of the beginning and puts it at the end; next he shifts some more matter from the middle to the preface; then he thinks it over.

It seems to him that it is too big, it wants condensation. The scientific world will say he has made too much of it; it ought to read very slight, and present the facts while concealing the labour. So he sets about removing the superfluous — leaves out all the personal observations, and all the little adventures he has met with in his investigations; and so, having got it down to the dry bones and stones thereof, and omitted all the mortar that stuck them together, he sends for the engraver, and the next three years are occupied in working up the illustrations. About this time some new discovery is made by a foreign observer, which necessitates a complete revision of the subject; and so having shifted the contents of the book about hither and thither till he does not know which is the end and which is the beginning, he pitches the much-mutilated copy into a drawer and turns the key. Farewell, no more of this; his declining days shall be spent in peace. A few months afterwards a work is announced in Leipsic which 'really trenches on my favourite subject, and really after spending a lifetime I can't stand it'. By this time his handwriting has become so shaky he can hardly read it himself, so he sends in despair for a lady who works a typewriter, and with infinite patience she makes a clean manuscript of the muddled mass. To the press at last, and the proofs come rapidly. Such a relief! How joyfully easy a thing is when you set about it! but by and by this won't do. Subsection A ought to be in a footnote, family B is doubtful; and so the corrections grow and run over the margin in a thin treble hand, till they approach the bulk of the original book — a good profit for the printer; and so after about forty years the monograph is published — the work of a life is accomplished. Fifty copies are sent round to as many public libraries and learned societies, and the rest of the impression lies on the shelves till dust and time and spiders' webs have buried it. Splendid work in it too. Looked back upon from today with the key of modern thought, these monographs often contain a whole chest of treasure. And still there are the periodicals, a century of magazines and journals and reviews and notices that have been coming out these hundred years and dropping to the ground like dead leaves unnoticed. And then there are the art works — books about shape and colour and ornament, and a naturalist lately has been trying to see how the leaves of one tree look fitted on the boughs of another. Boundless is the wealth of Flora's lap; the ingenuity of man has been weaving wreaths out of it for ages, and still the bottom of the sack is not yet. Nor have we got much news of the dandelion. For I sit on the thrown timber under the trees and mediate, and I want something more: I want the soul of the flowers.

The bee and the butterfly take their pollen and their honey, and the strange moths so curiously coloured, like the curious colouring of the owls, come to them by night, and they turn towards the sun and live their little day, and their petals fall, and where is the soul when the body decays? I want the inner meaning and the understanding of the wild flowers in the meadow. Why are they? What end? What purpose? The plant knows, and sees, and feels; where is its mind when the petal falls? Absorbed in the universal dynamic force, or what? They make no shadow of pretence, these beautiful flowers, of being beautiful for my sake, of bearing honey for me; in short, there does not seem to be any kind of relationship between us, and yet — as I said just now — language does not express the dumb feelings of the mind any more than the flower can speak. I want to know the soul of the flowers, but the word soul does not in the smallest degree convey the meaning of my wish. It is quite inadequate; I must hope that you will grasp the drift of my meaning. All these life-laboured monographs, these classifications, works of Linnaeus, and our own classic Darwin, microscope, physiology, and the flower has not given us its message yet. There are a million books; there are no books: all the books have to be written. What a field! A whole million of books have got to be written. In this sense there are hardly a dozen of them done, and these mere primers. The thoughts of man are like the foraminifera, those minute shells which build up the solid chalk hills and lay the level plain of endless sand; so minute that, save with a powerful lens, you would never imagine the dust on your fingers to be more than dust. The thoughts of man are like these: each to him seems great in his day, but the ages roll, and they shrink till they become triturated dust, and you might, as it were, put a thousand on your thumb-nail. They are not shapeless dust for all that; they are organic, and they build and weld and grow together, till in the passage of time they will make a new earth and a new life. So I think I may say there are no books; the books are yet to be written.

Let us get a little alchemy out of the dandelions. They are not precise, the Arabian sages, with their flowing robes and handwriting; there was a large margin to their manuscripts, much imagination. Therein they failed, judged by the monograph standard, but gave a subtle food for the mind. Some of this I would fain see now inspiring the works and words of our great men of science and thought — a little alchemy. A great change is slowly going forward all over the printing-press world, I mean wherever men print books and papers. The Chinese are perhaps outside that world at present, and the other Asian races; the myriads, too, of the great southern islands and of Africa. The change is steadily, however, proceeding wherever the printing-press is used. Nor Pope, nor Kaiser, nor Czar, nor Sultan, nor fanatic monk, nor meuzzin, shouting in vain from his minaret, nor, most fanatic of all, the fanatic shouting in vain in London, can keep it out — all powerless against a bit of printed paper. Bits of printed paper that listen to no command, to which none can say, 'Stand back; thou shalt not enter.' They rise on the summer whirlwinds from the very dust of the road, and float over the highest walls; they fall on the well-kept lawns — monastery, prison, palace — there is no fortress against a bit of printed paper. They penetrate where even Danaë's gold cannot go. Our Darwins, our Lyalls, Herschels, Faradays — all the immense army of those that go down to nature with considering eye — are steadfastly undermining and obliterating the superstitious past, literally burying it under endless loads of accumulated facts; and the printing-presses, like so many Argos, take these facts on their voyage round the world. Over go temples, and minarets, and churches, or rather there they stay, the hollow shells, like the snail shells which thrushes have picked clean; there they stay like Karnac, where there is no more incense, like the stone circles on our own hills, where there are no more human sacrifices. Thus men's minds all over the printing-press world are unlearning the falsehoods that have bound them down so long; they are unlearning, the first step to learn. They are going down to nature and

taking up the clods with their own hands, and so coming to have touch of that which is real. As yet we are in the fact stage; by and by we shall come to the alchemy, and get the honey for the inner mind and soul. I found, therefore, from the dandelion that there were no books, and it came upon me, believe me, as a great surprise, for I had lived quite certain that I was surrounded with them. It is nothing but unlearning, I find now; five thousand books to unlearn.

Then to unlearn the first ideas of history, of science, of social institutions, to unlearn one's own life and purpose; to unlearn the old mode of thought and way of arriving at things; to take off peel after peel, and so get by degrees slowly towards the truth — thus writing as it were, a sort of floating book in the mind, almost remaking the soul. It seems as if the chief value of books is to give us something to unlearn. Sometimes I feel indignant at the false views that were instilled into me in early days, and then again I see that that very indignation gives me a moral life. I hope in the days to come future thinkers will unlearn us, and find ideas infinitely better. How marvellous it seems that there should be found communities furnished with the printing-press and fully convinced they are more intelligent than ants, and yet deliberately refusing by a solid 'popular' vote to accept free libraries! They look with scorn on the mediaeval times, when volumes were chained in the college library or to the desk at church. Ignorant times those! A good thing it would be if only three books were chained to a desk, open and free in every parish throughout the kingdom now. So might the wish to unlearn be at last started in the inert mind of the mass. Almost the only books left to me to read, and not to unlearn very much, are my first books — the graven classics of Greece and Rome, cut with a stylus so deeply into the tablet they cannot be erased. Little of the monograph or of classification, no bushel of baskets full of facts, no minute dissection of nature, no attempt to find the soul under the scalpel. Thoughts which do not exactly deal with nature direct in a mechanical way, as the chemist labels all his gums and spices and earths in small boxes — I wonder if anybody at Athens every made a collection of the coleoptera? Yet in some way they had got the spirit of the earth and sea, the soul of the sun. This never dies; this I wish not to unlearn; this is ever fresh and beautiful as a summer morning:-

> Such the golden crocus,
> Fair flower of early spring; the gopher white,
> And fragrant thyme, and all the unsown beauty
> Which in moist grounds the verdant meadows bear;
> The ox-eye, the sweet-smelling flower of Jove,
> The chalca, and the much-sung hyacinth,
> And the low-growing violet, to which
> Dark Proserpine a darker hue has given.

They come nearest to our own violets and cowslips — the unsown beauty of our meadows — to the hawthorn leaf and the high pinewood. I can forget all else that I have read, but it is difficult to forget these even when I will. I read them in English. I had the usual Latin and Greek instruction, but I read them in English deliberately. For the inflexion of the vowel I care nothing; I prize the idea. Scholars may regard me with scorn. I reply with equal scorn. I say that a great classic thought is greater to an English mind in English words than in any other form, and therein fits best to this our life and day. I read them in English first, and intend to do so to the end. I do not know what set me on these books, but I began them when about eighteen. The first of all was Diogenes Laertius's *Lives of the Philosophers.* It was a happy choice; my good genius, I suppose, for you see I was already fairly well read in modern science, and these old Greek philosophers set me thinking backwards, unwinding and unlearning, and getting at that eidolon which is not to be found in the mechanical heavens of this age. I still read him. I still find new things, quite new, because they are so very, very old, and quite true; and with his help I seem in a measure to look back upon our thoughts now as if I had projected myself a thousand years forward in space. An imperfect book, say the critics. I do not know about that; his short paragraphs and chapters in their imperfect state convey more freshness to the mind than the thick, laboured volumes in which modern scholarship professes to describe ancient philosophy. I prefer the imperfect original records. Neither can I read the ponderous volumes of modern history, which are nothing but words. I prefer the incomplete and shattered chronicles themselves, where the swords shine and the armour rings, and all is life though but a broken frieze. Next came Plato (it took me a long time to read Plato, and I have had to unlearn much of him) and Xenophon. Socrates' dialectic method taught me how to write, or rather how to put ideas in sequence. Sophocles, too; and last, that wonderful encyclopaedia of curious things, Athenaeus. So that I found, when the idea of the hundred best books came out, that between seventy and eighty of them had been my companions almost from boyhood, those lacking to complete the number being chiefly ecclesiastical or Continental. Indeed, some years before the hundred books were talked of, the idea had occurred to me of making up a catalogue of books that could be bought for ten pounds. In an article in the *Pall Mall Gazette* on 'The Pigeons of the British Museum' I said, 'It seems as if all the books in the world — really books — can be bought for £10. Man's whole thought is purchasable at that small price — for the value of a watch, of a good dog.' The idea of making a £10 catalogue was in my mind — I did make a rough pencil one — and I still think that a £10 library is worth the notice of the publishing world. My rough list did not contain a hundred. These old books of nature and nature's mind ought to be chained up, free for every man to read in every parish. These are the only books I do not wish to unlearn, one item only expected, which I shall not here discuss. It is curious, too, that the Greek philosophers, in the more rigid sense of science, anticipated most of the drift of modern thought. Two chapters in Aristotle might almost be printed without change as summaries of our present natural science. For the facts of nature, of course, neither one hundred books nor a £10 library would be worth mentioning; say five thousand, and having read those, then go to Kew, and spend a year studying the specimens of wood only stored there, such a little slice after all of the whole. You will then believe what I have advanced, that there are no books as yet; they have got to be written; and if we pursue the idea a little further, and consider that these are all about the crude clods of life

— for I often feel what a very crude and clumsy clod I am — only of the earth, a minute speck among one hundred millions of stars, how shall we write what is *there*? It is only to be written by the mind or soul, and that is why I strive so much to find what I have called the alchemy of nature. Let us not be too entirely mechanical, Baconian and experimental only; let us let the soul hope and dream and float on these oceans of accumulated facts, and feel still greater aspiration than it has ever known since first a flint was chipped before the glaciers. Man's mind is the most important fact with which we are yet acquainted. Let us not turn then against it and deny its existence with too many brazen statements, but remember these are but a means, and that the vast lens of the Californian refractor is but glass — it is the infinite speck upon which the ray of light will fall that is the one great fact of the universe. By the mind, without instruments, the Greeks anticipated almost all our thoughts; by and by, having raised ourselves up upon these huge mounds of facts, we shall begin to see still greater things; to do so we must look not at the mound underfoot, but at the starry horizon.

Fortnightly Review, 1 May 1887

Just Before Winter

A RICH tint of russet deepened on the forest top, and seemed to sink day by day deeper into the foliage like a stain; riper and riper it grew, as an apple colours. Broad acres these of the last crop, the crop of leaves; a thousand thousand quarters, the broad earth will be their barn. A warm red lies on the hillside above the woods, as if the red dawn stayed there through the day; it is the heath and heather seeds; and higher still, a pale yellow fills the larches. The whole of the great hill glows with colour under the short hours of the October sun; and overhead, where the pine cones hang, the sky is of the deepest azure. The conflagration of the woods burning luminously crowds into those short hours a brilliance the slow summer does not know.

The frosts and mists and battering rains that follow in quick succession after the equinox, the chill winds that creep about the fields, have ceased a little while, and there is a pleasant sound in the fir trees. Everything is not gone yet. In the lanes that lead down to the 'shaws' in the dells, the 'gills,' as these wooded depths are called, buckler ferns, green, fresh, and elegantly fashioned, remain under the shelter of the hazel-lined banks. From the tops of the ash wands, where the linnets so lately sang, coming up from the stubble, the darkened leaves have been blown, and their much-divided branches stand bare like outstretched fingers. Black-spotted sycamore leaves are down, but the moss grows thick and deeply green; and the trumpets of the lichen seem to be larger, now they are moist, than when they were dry under the summer heat. Here is herb

Robert in flower — its leaves are scarlet; a leaf of St. John's-wort, too, has become scarlet; the bramble leaves are many shades of crimson; one plant of tormentil has turned yellow. Furze bushes, grown taller since the spring, bear a second bloom, but not perhaps so golden as the first. It is the true furze, and not the lesser gorse; it is covered with half-opened buds; and it is clear if the short hours of sun would but lengthen, the whole gorse hedge would become aglow again. Our trees, too, that roll up their buds so tightly, like a dragoon's cloak, would open them again at Christmas; and the sticky horse chestnut would send forth its long ears of leaves for New Year's Day. They would all come out in leaf again if we had but a little more sun; *they* are quite ready for a second summer.

Brown lie the acorns, yellow where they were fixed in their cups; two of these cups seem almost as large as the great acorns from abroad. A red dead-nettle, a mauve thistle, white and pink bramble flowers, a white strawberry, a little yellow tormentil, a broad yellow dandelion, narrow hawkweeds, and blue scabious, are all in flower in the lane. Others are scattered on the mounds and in the meads adjoining, where may be collected some heath still in bloom, prunella, hypericum, white yarrow, some heads of red clover, some beautiful buttercups, three bits of blue veronica, wild chamomile, tall yellow-weed, pink centaury, succory, dock cress, daisies, fleabane, knapweed, and delicate blue harebells. Two York roses flower on the hedge: altogether, twenty-six flowers, a large bouquet for October 19, gathered, too, in a hilly country.

Besides these, note the broad hedge-parsley leaves, tunnelled by leaf-miners; bright masses of haws gleaming in the sun; scarlet hips; great brown cones fallen from the spruce firs; black heart-shaped bindweed leaves here, and buff bryony leaves yonder; green and scarlet berries of white bryony hanging thickly on bines from which the leaves have withered; and bunches of grass, half yellow and half green, along the mound. Now that the leaves have been brushed from the beech saplings you may see how the leading stem rises in a curious wavy line; some of the leaves lie at the foot, washed in white dew, that stays in the shade all day; and wetness of the dew makes the brownish red of the leaf show clear and bright. One leaf falls in the stillness of the air slowly, as if let down by a cord of gossamer gently, and not as a stone falls — fate delayed to the last. A moth adheres to a bough, his wings half open, like a short brown cloak flung over his shoulders. Pointed leaves, some drooping, some horizontal, some fluttering slightly, still stay on the tall willow wands, like bannerets on the knights' lances, much torn in the late battle of the winds. There is a shower from a clear sky under the trees in the forest; brown acorns rattling as they fall, and rich coloured Spanish chestnuts thumping the sward, and sometimes striking you as you pass under; they lie on the ground in pocketfuls. Specks of brilliant scarlet dot the grass like some bright berries blown from the bushes; but on stooping to pick them, they are found to be the heads of a fungus. Near by lies a black magpie's feather, spotted with round dots of white.

At the edge of the trees stands an old timbered farmstead, whose gables and dark lines of wood have not been painted in the memory of man, dull and weather-beaten, but very homely; and by it rises the delicate cone of a new oast-house, the tiles on which are of the brightest red. Lines of bluish smoke ascend from among the bracken of the wild open ground, where a tribe of gipsies have pitched their camp. Three of the vans are time-stained and travel-worn, with dull red roofs; the fourth is brightly picked out with fresh yellow paint, and stands a marked object at the side. Orange-red beeches rise beyond them on the slope; two hoop-tents, or kibitkas, just large enough to creep into, are near the fires, where the women are cooking the gipsy's bouillon, that savoury stew of all things good: vegetables, meat, scraps and savouries collected as it were in the stockpot from twenty miles round. Hodge, the stay-at-home, sturdy carter, eats bread and cheese and poor bacon sometimes; he looks with true British scorn on all scraps and soups, and stockpots and bouillons — not for him, not he; he would rather munch dry bread and cheese for every meal all the year round, though he could get bits as easy as the other and without begging. The gipsy is a cook. The man with a gold ring in his ear; the woman with a silver ring on her finger, coarse

black snaky hair like a horse's mane; the boy with naked olive feet; dark eyes all of them, and an Oriental, sidelong look and a strange inflection of tone that turns our common English words into a foreign language — there they camp in the fern, in the sun, their Eastern donkeys of Syria scattered round them, their children rolling about like foals in the grass, a bit out of the distant Orient under our Western oaks.

It is the nature of the oak to be still, it is the nature of the hawk to roam with the wind. The Anglo-Saxon labourer remains in his cottage generation after generation, ploughing the same fields; the express train may rush by, but he feels no wish to rush with it; he scarcely turns to look at it; all the note he takes is that it marks the time to 'knock off' and ride the horses home. And if hard want to last forces him away, and he emigrates, he would as soon jog to the port in a waggon, a week on the road, as go by steam; as soon voyage in a sailing ship as by the swift Cunarder. The swarthy gipsy, like the hawk, for ever travels on, but, like the hawk, that seems to have no road and yet returns to the same trees, so he, winding in circles of which we civilised people do not understand the map, comes, in his own times and seasons, home to the same waste spot, and cooks his savoury bouillon by the same beech. They have camped here for so many years that it is impossible to trace when they did not; it is wild still, like themselves. Nor has their nature changed any more than the nature of the trees.

The gipsy loves the crescent moon, the evening star, the clatter of the fern-owl, the beetle's hum. He was born on the earth in the tent, and he has lived like a species of human wild animal ever since. Of his own free will he will have nothing to do with rites or litanies: he may perhaps be married in a place of worship — to make it legal, that is all. At the end, were it not for the law, he would for choice be buried beneath the 'fireplace' of their children's children. He will not dance to the pipe ecclesiastic, sound it who may — Churchman, Dissenter, priest, or laic. Like the trees, he is simply indifferent. All the great wave of teaching and text and tracts and missions and the produce of the printing-press has made no impression upon his race any more than upon the red deer that roam in the forest behind his camp. The negroes have their fetich, every nation its idols; the gipsy alone has none — not even a superstitious observance; they have no idolatry of the Past, neither have they the exalted thought of the Present. It is very strange that it should be so at this the height of our civilisation, and you might go many thousand miles and search from Africa to Australia before you would find another people without a Deity. That can only be seen under an English sky, under English oaks and beeches.

Are they the oldest race on earth? and have they worn out all the gods? Have they worn out all the hopes and fears of the human heart in tens of thousands of years, and do they merely live, acquiescent to fate? For some have thought to trace in the older races an apathy as with the Chinese, a religion of moral maxims and some few joss-house superstitions, which they themselves full well know to be nought, worshipping their ancestors, but with no vital living force, like that which drove Mohammed's bands to zealous fury, like that which sent our own Puritans over the sea in the *Mayflower*. No living faith. So old, so very, very old, older than the Chinese, older than the Copts of Egypt, older than the Aztecs; back to those dim Sanskrit times that seem like the clouds on the far horizon of human experience, where space and chaos begin to take shape, though but of vapour. So old, they went through civilisation ten thousand years since; they have worn it all out, even hope in the future; they merely live acquiescent to fate, like the red deer. The crescent moon, the evening star, the clatter of the fern-owl, the red embers of the wood fire, the pungent smoke blown round about by the occasional puffs of wind, the shadowy trees, the sound of the horses cropping the grass, the night that steals on till the stubbles alone are light among the fields — the gipsy sleeps in his tent on mother earth; it is, you see, primeval man with primeval nature. One thing he gains at least — an iron health, an untiring foot, women whose haunches bear any burden, children whose naked feet are not afraid of the dew.

By sharp contrast, the Anglo-Saxon labourer who lives in the cottage close by and works at the old timbered farmstead is profoundly religious.

The gipsies return from their rambling soon after the end of hop-picking, and hold a kind of informal fair on the village green with

cockshies, swings, and all the clumsy games that extract money from clumsy hands. It is almost the only time of the year when the labouring people have any cash; their weekly wages are mortgaged beforehand; the hop-picking money comes in a lump, and they have something to spend. Hundreds of pounds are paid to meet the tally or account kept by the pickers, the old word tally still surviving, and this had to be charmed out of their pockets. Besides the gipsies' fair, the little shopkeepers in the villages send out circulars to the most outlying cottage announcing the annual sale at an immense sacrifice; anything to get the hop-pickers' cash; and the packmen come round, too, with jewelry and lace and finery. The village by the forest has been haunted by the gipsies for a century; its population in the last thirty years has much increased, and it is very curious to observe how the gipsy element has impregnated the place. Not only are the names gipsy, the faces are gipsy; the black coarse hair, high cheek-bones, and peculiar forehead linger; even many of the shopkeepers have a distinct trace, and others that do not show it so much are known to be nevertheless related.

Until land became so valuable — it is now again declining — these forest grounds of heath and bracken were free to all comers, and great numbers of squatters built huts and inclosed pieces of land. They cleared away the gorse and heath and grubbed the fir-tree stumps, and found, after a while, that the apparently barren sand could grow a good sward. No-one would think anything could flourish on such an arid sand, exposed at a great height on the open hill to the cutting winds. Contrary, however, to appearances, fair crops, and sometimes two crops of hay are yielded, and there is always a good bite for cattle. These squatters consequently came to keep cows, sometimes one and sometimes two — anticipating the three acres and a cow; and it is very odd to hear the women at the hop-picking telling each other they are going to churn tonight. They have, in fact, little dairies. Such are the better class of squatters. But others there are who have shown no industry, half-gipsies, who do anything but work — tramp, beg, or poach; sturdy fellows, stalking round with toy-brooms for sale, with all the blackguardism of both races. They keep just within the law; they do not steal or commit burglary; but decency, order and society they set utterly at defiance. For instance, a gentleman pleased with the splendid view built a large mansion in one spot, never noticing that the entrance was opposite a row of cottages, or rather thinking no evil of it. The result was that neither his wife nor visitors could go in or out without being grossly insulted, without rhyme or reason, merely for the sake of blackguardism. Now, the pure gipsy in his tent or the Anglo-Saxon labourer would not do this; it was the half-breed. The original owner was driven from his premises; and they are said to have changed hands several times since from the same cause. All over the parish this half-breed element shows its presence by the extraordinary and unusual coarseness of manner. The true English rustic is always civil, however rough, and will not offend you with anything unspeakable, so that at first it is quite bewildering to meet with such behaviour in the midst of green lanes. This is the explanation — the gipsy taint. Instead of the growing population obliterating the gipsy, the gipsy has saturated the English folk.

When people saw the red man driven from the prairies and backwoods of America, and whole states as large as Germany without a single Indian left, much was written on the extermination of the aborigines by the stronger Saxon. As the generations lengthen, the facts appear to wear another aspect. From the intermarriage of the lower orders with the Indian squaws the Indian blood has got into the Saxon veins, and now the cry is that the red man is exterminating the Saxon, so greatly has he leavened the population. The typical Yankee face, as drawn in *Punch*, is indeed the red Indian profile with a white skin and a chimney-pot hat. Upon a small scale the same thing has happened in this village by the forest; the gipsy half-breed has stained the native blood. Perhaps races like the Jew and gipsy, so often quoted as instances of the permanency of type, really owe that apparent fixity to their power of mingling with other nations. They are kept alive as races by mixing; otherwise one or two things would happen — the Jew and the gipsy must have died out, or else have supplanted all the races of the globe. Had the Jews been so fixed a type, by this time their offspring would have been more numerous than the Chinese. The reverse, however, is the case; and therefore we may suppose they must have become extinct, had it not been for fresh supplies of Saxon, Teuton, Spanish and Italian blood. It is, in fact, the intermarriages that have kept the falsely so-called pure races of these human parasites alive. The mixing is continually going on. The gipsies who still stay in their tents, however, look askance upon those who desert them for the roof. Two gipsy women, thoroughbred, came into a village shop and bought a variety of groceries, ending with a pound of biscuits and a Guy Fawkes mask for a boy. They were clad in dirty jackets and hats, draggle-tails, unkempt and unwashed, with orange and red kerchiefs round their necks (the gipsy colours). Happening to look out of the window, they saw a young servant girl with a perambulator on the opposite side of the 'street'; she was tidy and decently dressed, looking after her mistress's children in civilised fashion; but they recognised her as a deserter from the tribe, and blazed with contempt. 'Don't *she* look a figure!' exclaimed these dirty creatures.

The short hours shorten, and the leaf-crop is gathered to the great barn of the earth; the oaks alone, more tenacious, retain their leaves, that have now become a colour like new leather. It is too brown for buff — it is more like fresh harness. The berries are red on the holly bushes and holly trees that grow, whole copses of them, on the forest slopes — 'The Great Rough'; the half-wild sheep have polished the stems of these holly trees till they shine, by rubbing their fleeces against them. The farmers have been drying their damp wheat in the oast-houses over charcoal fires, and wages are lowered, and men discharged. Vast loads of brambles and thorns, dead firs, useless hop-poles and hop-bines, and gorse are drawn together for the great bonfire on the green. The 5th of November bonfires are still vital institutions, and from the top of the hill you may see them burning in all directions, as if an enemy had set fire to the hamlets.

Chamber's Journal, 18 December 1886

Summer in Somerset

THE BROWN Barle River running over red rocks aslant its course is pushed aside, and races round curving slopes. The first shoot of the rapid is smooth and polished like a gem by the lapidary's art, rounded and smooth as a fragment of torso, and this convex undulation maintains a solid outline. Then the following scoop under is furrowed as if ploughed across, and the ridge of each furrow, where the particles move a little less swiftly than in the hollow of the groove, falls backwards as foam blown from a wave. At the foot of the furrowed decline the current rises over a rock in a broad white sheet — white because as it is dashed to pieces the air mingles with it. After this furious haste the stream does but just overtake those bubbles which have been carried along on another division of the water flowing steadily but straight. Sometimes there are two streams like this between the same banks, sometimes three or even more, each running at a different rate, and each gliding above a floor differently inclined. The surface of each of these streams slopes in a separate direction, and though under the same light they reflect it at varying angles. The river is animated and alive, rushing here, gliding there, foaming yonder; its separate and yet component parallels striving together, and talking loudly in incomplete sentences. Those rivers that move through midland meads present a broad, calm surface, at the same level from side to side; they flow without sound, and if you stood behind a thick hedge you would not know that a river was near. They dream along the meads, toying with their forget-me-nots, too idle even to make love to their flowers vigorously. The brown Barle enjoys his life, and splashes in the sunshine like boys bathing — like them he is sunburnt and brown. He throws the wanton spray over the ferns that bow and bend as the cool breeze his current brings sways them in the shade. He laughs and talks, and sings louder than the wind in his woods.

Here is a pool by the bank under an ash — a deep green pool inclosed by massive rocks, which the stream has to brim over. The water is green — or is it the ferns, and the moss, and the oaks, and the pale ash reflected? This rock has a purple tint, dotted with moss spots almost black; the green water laps at the purple stone, and there is one place where a thin line of scarlet is visible, though I do not know what causes it. Another stone the spray does not touch has been dried to a bright white by the sun. Inclosed, the green water slowly swirls round till it finds crevices, and slips through. A few paces farther up there is a red rapid — reddened stones, and reddened growths beneath the water, a light that lets the red hues overcome the others — a wild rush of crowded waters rotating as they go, shrill voices calling. The next bend upwards dazzles the eyes, for every inclined surface and striving parallel, every swirl, and bubble, and eddy, and rush around a rock chances to reflect the sunlight. Not one long pathway of quiet sheen, such as stretches across a rippled lake, each wavelet throwing back its ray in just proportion, but a hundred separate mirrors vibrating, each inclined at a different angle, each casting a tremulous flash into the face. The eyelids involuntarily droop to shield the gaze from a hundred arrows; they are too strong — nothing can be distinguished but a woven surface of brilliance, a mesh of light, under which the water runs, itself invisible. I will go back to the deep green pool, and walking now with the sun behind, how the river has changed!

Soft, cool shadows reached over it, which I did not see before; green surfaces are calm under trees; the rocks are less hard; the stream runs more gently, and the oaks come down nearer; the delicious sound of the rushing water almost quenches my thirst. My eyes have less work to do to meet the changing features of the current which now seems smooth as

'A pheasant crows'

my glance accompanies its movement. The sky, which was not noticed before, now appears reaching in rich azure across the deep hollow, from the oaks on one side to the oaks on the other. These woods, which cover the steep and rocky walls of the gorge from river to summit, are filled with the June colour of oak. It is not green, nor russet, nor yellow; I think it may be called a glow of yellow under green. It is warmer than green; the glow is not on the outer leaves, but comes up beneath from the depth of the branches. The rush of the river soothes the mind, and broad descending surfaces of yellow-green oak carry the glance downwards from the blue over to the stream in the hollow. Rush! rush! — it is the river, like a mightly wind in the wood. A pheasant crows, and once and again falls the tap, tap of woodmen's axes — scarce heard, for they are high above. They strip the young oaks of their bark as far as they can while the saplings stand, then fell them, and as they all lie downhill there are parallel streaks of buff (where the sap has dried) drawn between the yellow-green masses of living leaf. The pathway winds in among the trees at the base of the rocky hill; light green whortleberries fill every interstice, bearing tiny red globes of flower — flower-lamps — open at the top. Wood-sorrel lifts its delicate veined petals; the leaf is rounded like the shadow of a bubble on the stone under clear water. I like to stay by the wood-sorrel a little while — it is so chastely beautiful; like the purest verse, it speaks to the inmost heart. Staying, I hear unconsciously — listen! Rush! rush! like a mighty wind in the woods.

It draws me on to the deep green pool inclosed about by rocks — a pool to stand near and think into. The purple rock, dotted with black moss; the white rock; the thin scarlet line; the green water; the overhanging tree; the verdant moss upon the bank; the lady fern — are there still. But I see also now a little pink somewhere in the water, much brown too, and shades I know no name for. The water is not green, but holds in solution three separate sets of colours. The confervae on the stones, the growths beneath at the bottom waving a little as the water swirls like minute seaweeds — these are brown and green and somewhat reddish too. Underwater the red rock is toned and paler, but has deep

black cavities. Next, the surface, continually changing as it rotates, throws back a different light, and thirdly, the oaks' yellow-green high up, the pale ash, the tender ferns drooping over low down confer their tints on the stream. So from the floor of the pool, from the surface, and from the adjacent bank, three sets of colours mingle. Washed together by the slow swirl, they produce a shade — the brown of the Barle — lost in darkness where the bank overhangs.

Following the current downwards at last the river for a while flows in quietness, broad and smooth. A trout leaps for a fly with his tail curved in the air, full a foot out of water. Trout watch behind sunken stones, and shoot to and fro as insects droop in their flight and appear about to fall. So clear is the water and so brightly illuminated that the fish are not easily seen — for vision depends on contrast — but in a minute I find a way to discover them by their shadows. The black shadow of a trout is distinct upon the bottom of the river, and guides the eye to the spot; then looking higher in the transparent water there is the fish. It was curious to see these black shadows darting to and fro as if themselves animated and without bodies, for if the trout darted before being observed the light concealed him in motion. Some of the trout came up

from under Torre-steps, a singular structure which here connects the shores of the stream. Every one has seen a row of stepping-stones across a shallow brook; now pile other stones on each of these, forming buttresses, and lay flat stones like unhewn planks from buttress to buttress, and you have the plan of this primitive bridge. It has a megalithic appearance, as if associated with the age of rude stone monuments. They say its origin is doubtful; there can be no doubt of the loveliness of the spot. The Barle comes with his natural rush and fierceness under the unhewn stone planking, then deepens, and there overhanging a black pool — for the shadow was so deep as to be black — grew a large bunch of marsh-marigolds in fullest flower, the broad golden cups almost resting on the black water. The bridge is not intended for wheels, and though it is as firm as the rock, foot passengers have to look at their steps, as the great planks, flecked with lichen at the edges, are not all level. The horned sheep and lambs go over it — where do they not go? Like goats they wander everywhere.

In a cottage some way up the hill we ate clotted cream and whortleberry jam. Through the open door came the ceaseless rush! rush! like a wind in the wood. The floor was of concrete, lime and sand; on the open hearth — pronounced 'airth' — sods of turf cut from the moor and oak branches were smouldering under the chimney crook. Turf smoke from the piled-up fires of winter had darkened the beams of the ceiling, but from that rude room there was a view of the river, and the hill, and the oaks in full June colour, which the rich would envy. Sometimes in early morning the wild red deer are seen feeding on the slope opposite. As we drove away in reckless Somerset style, along precipices above the river, with nothing but a fringe of fern for parapet, the oak woods on the hills under us were shading down into evening coolness of tint, the yellow less warm, the green more to the surface. Upon the branches of the trees moss grows, forming a level green top to the round bough like a narrow cushion along it, with frayed edges drooping over each side. Though moss is common on branches, it does not often make a raised cushion, thick, as if green velvet pile were laid for the birds to run on. There were rooks' nests in some tall ash trees; the scanty foliage left the nests exposed, they were still occupied by late broods. Rooks' nests are not often seen in ashes as in elms.

By a mossy bank a little girl — a miniature Audrey — stout, rosy and ragged, stood with a yellow straw hat aslant on her yellow hair, eating the leaves from a spray of beech in her hand. Audrey looked at us, eating the beech leaves steadily, but would not answer, not even 'Where's your father to?' For in Somerset the 'to' is put last, and must never be omitted; thus, instead of saying 'I bought this at Taunton', it is correct to say 'I bought this to Taunton.' There are models under glass cases in places of entertainment with a notice to say that if a penny be inserted the machine will go. Audrey the Little would not speak, but when a penny was put in her hand she began to move, and made off for home with the treasure. The road turned and turned, but whichever way the Barle was always under us, and the red rock rose high at the side. This rock fractures aslant if worked, vast flakes come out, and the cleavage is so natural that until closely approached a quarry appears a cliff. Stone got out in squares, or cut down straight, leaves an artificial wall; these rocks cannot be made to look artificial, and if painted a quarry would be certainly quite indistinguishable from a natural precipice. Entering a little town (Dulverton) the road is jammed tight between cottages: so narrow is the lane that foot passengers huddle up in doorways to avoid the touch of the wheels, and the windows of the houses are protected by iron bars like cages lest the splash-boards should crack the glass. Nowhere in closest-built London is there such a lane — one would imagine land to be dear indeed. The farm labourers, filing homewards after their day's work, each carry poles of oak or faggots on their shoulders for their hearths, generally oak branches; it is their perquisite. The oak somehow takes root among the interstices of the stones of this rocky land. Past the houses the rush! rush! of the brown Barle rises again in the still evening air.

From the Devon border I drifted like a leaf detached from a tree, across to a deep coomb in the Quantock Hills. The vast hollow is made for repose and lotus-eating; its very shape, like a hammock, indicates idleness. There the days go over noiselessly and without effort, like white summer clouds. Ridges each side rise high and heroically steep — it would be proper to set out and climb them, but not today, not now: some time presently. To the left massive Will's Neck stands out in black shadow defined and distinct, like a fragment of night in the bright light of the day. The wild red deer lie there, but the mountain is afar; a sigh is all I can give to it, for the Somerset sun is warm and the lotus sweet. Yonder, if the misty heat moves on, the dim line of Dunkery winds along the sky, not unlike the curved black of a crouching hare. The weight of the mountains is too great — what is the use of attempting to move? It is enough to look at them. The day goes over like a white cloud; as the sun declines it is pleasant to go into the orchard — the vineyard of Somerset, and then perhaps westward may be seen a light in the sky by the horizon as if thrown up from an immense mirror under. The mirror is the Severn sea, itself invisible at this depth, but casting a white glow up against the vapour in the air. By it you may recognise the nearness of the sea. The thumbnail ridges of the Quantocks begin to grow harder, they carry the eye along on soft curves like those of the South Downs in Sussex, but suddenly end in a flourish and point as if cut out with the thumbnail. Draw your thumbnail firmly along soft wood, and it will, by its natural slip,. form such a curve. Blackbird and thrush commence to sing as the heavy heat decreases; the bloom on the apple trees is loose now, and the blackbird as he springs from the bough shakes down flakes of blossom.

Towards even a wind moves among the lengthening shadows, and my footsteps involuntarily seek the glen, where a streamlet trickles down over red flat stones which resound musically as the water strikes them. Ferns are growing so thickly in the hedge that soon it will seem composed of their fronds; the first June rose hangs above their green tips. A water-ousel with white breast rises and flies on; again disturbed, he makes a circle, and returns to the stream behind. On the moist earth there is the print of a hare's pad; here is a foxglove out in flower; and now as the incline rises heather thickens on the slope. Sometimes we wander beside the streamlet which goes a mile into the coomb — the shadow is deep and cool in the vast groove of the hill, the shadow accumulates there, and is pressed by its own weight — up slowly as far as the 'sog', or peaty place where the spring rises, and where the sundew grows. Sometimes climbing steep and rocky walls — scarce sprinkled with grass — we pause every other minute to look down on the great valley which reaches across to Dunkery. The horned sheep, which are practically wild, like wild creatures, have worn out holes for themselves to lie in beside the hill. If resolution is strong, we move through the dark heather (soon to be purple), startling the heath-poults, or black game, till at last the Channel

opens, and the far-distant Flat and Steep Holms lie, as it looks, afloat on the dim sea. This is labour enough; stern indeed must be the mind that could work at summer's noon in Somerset, when the apple vineyards slumber; when the tall foxgloves stand in the heavy heat and the soft air warms the deepest day-shadow so that nothing is cool to the touch but the ferns. Is there anything so good as to do nothing?

Fame travels slowly up these breathless hills, and pauses overcome in the heated hollow lanes. A famous wit of European reputation, when living, resided in Somerset. A traveller one day chancing to pass through the very next parish inquired of a local man if somebody called Sydney Smith did not once live in that neighbourhood. 'Yes,' was the reply, 'I've heard all about Sydney Smith; I can tell you. He was a highwayman, and was hung on that hill there.' He would have shown the very stump of the gallows-tree as proof positive, like Jack Cade's bricks, alive in the chimney to this day.

There really was a highwayman, however, whose adventures are said to have suggested one of the characters in the romance of 'Lorna Doone'. This desperate fellow had of course his houses of call, where he could get refreshment safely, on the moors. One bitter winter's day the robber sat down to a hearty dinner in an inn at Exford. Placing his pistols before him, he made himself comfortable, and ate and drank his fill. By and by an old woman entered, and humbly took a seat in a corner far from the fire. In time the highwayman observed the wretched, shivering creature, and of his princely generosity told her to come and sit by the hearth. The old woman gladly obeyed, and crouched beside him. Presently, as he sat absorbed in his meal, his arms were suddenly pinioned from behind. The old woman had him tight, so that he could not use his weapons, while at a call constables, who had been posted about, rushed in and secured him. The old woman was in fact a man in disguise. A relation of the thief-taker still lives and tells the tale. The highwayman's mare, mentioned in the novel, had been trained to come at his call, and was so ungovernable that they shot her.

Such tracts of open country, moors, and unenclosed hills were the haunts of highwaymen till a late period, and memories of the gallows, and of escapes from them are common. A well-to-do farmer who used to attend Bristol market, and dispose there of large quantities of stock and produce, dared not bring home the money himself lest he should be robbed. He entrusted the cash to his drover; the farmer rode along the roads, the drover made short cuts on foot, and arrived safely with the money. This went on for years, in which time the honest fellow — a mere labourer — carried some thousands of pounds for his master, faithfully delivering every shilling. He had, however, a little failing — a dangerous one in those days, when the gallows was the punishment for sheep-stealing. He was known to be a sheep-stealer, and actually after bringing home a hundred pounds would go and put his neck in danger the very same night by taking a sheep. This went on for some time, people shut their eyes, but at last patience was exhausted, and efforts were made to catch him in the act, without success.

One night he came home in the usual manner from market, delivered the cash, and went to his cottage. Next day a little girl was sent on an innocent errand to the cottage, with orders while she was there to look sharply round and observe if there were any ashes on the floor. She came back with the news that there was a heap of wood ashes. Immediately a posse set out, and the drover was arrested. The use of the ashes by sheep-stealers was to suck up and remove stains of blood, which were certain to be left in cutting up the animal. Sufficient proof was found in the cottage to condemn the honest thief to be hung; great exertions were, however, made on his behalf; and principally, it is supposed, on account of his character for carrying large sums of money untouched, he was saved. There is a story of the smugglers — once notorious folk on these hills — teaching their horses to understand the usual words of command backwards. If they were driving packhorses along at night with a load of brandy landed from a lugger, and were met by the revenue men, who ordered them to stop that the packs might be searched, the smugglers, like good and loyal subjects, called 'Whoa! whoa!' Instantly the horses set off at a tearing gallop, for they understood 'Whoa!' as 'Gee-up!'

By a farmer's door I found a tall branch of oak lying against the porch. The bark was dry, and the leaves were shrivelled, but the bough had been originally taken green from the tree. These boughs are discovered against the door on the morning of the 28th of May, and are in memory of the escape of King Charles from his enemies by hiding in an oak. The village ringers leave them, and then go to the church and ring a peal, for which they expect cider or small coin from each loyal person honoured with an oak branch. Another custom, infinitely more ancient, is that of singing to the apple trees in early spring, so that the orchards may be induced to bear a good crop. The singers came round and visit each orchard; they have a rhyme especially for the purpose, part of the refrain of which is that a cup of good cider cannot do anyone harm — a hint which brings out a canful. In strange contrast to these genial customs, which accord so well with flowery fields, I heard an instance of the coldest indifference. An old couple lived for many years in a cottage; at last the wife died, and the husband, while the body was in the house, had his meals on the coffin as a table.

A hundred years since, before steam, the corn was threshed out by the flail — a slow, and consequently expensive process. Many efforts were made to thresh quicker. Among others, wooden machines were put up in some of the villages, something resembling a water-wheel placed horizontally. This was moved by horses walking round and round, and drove machinery in the barn by belt or shafting. The labourers, greatly incensed — for they regarded threshing by the flail as their right — tried to burn them, but the structures were guarded and still exist. Under the modern conditions of farming they are still found useful to cut chaff, crack corn, and so on. The ancient sickle is yet in use for reaping in Somerset; the reapers sharpen it by drawing the edge through an apple, when the acid bites and cleans the steel. While we were sauntering through a village one morning, out rushed the boys from school, and instantly their tongues began to wag of those things on which their hearts were set. 'I know a jay's nest,' said one; 'I know an owl's nest', cried a second; a third hastened to claim knowledge of a pigeon's nest. It will be long before education drives the natural love of the woods out of the children's hearts. Of old time a village school used to be held in an ancient building, the lower part of which was occupied as almshouses.

Underneath the ancient folk lived as best they might, while the young folk learned and gave their class responses, or romped on the floor overhead. The upper part of the building belonged to one owner, the lower part to another landlord. It came about that the roof decayed and the upper owner suggested to the lower owner that they should agree in bearing the cost of repairs. Upon which the owner of the basement remarked that he contemplated pulling his part down.

In these hamlets along the foot of the hills ancient stone crosses are often found. One of them has retained its top perfect, and really is a cross, not a shaft only. This is, I think, rare. Sometimes in the village street, the slender column grey against the green trees, sometimes in the churchyard, these crosses come on the mind like a sudden enigma. It requires an effort to grasp their meaning, so long have the ideas passed away which led to their erection. They almost startle modern thought. How many years since the peasant women knelt at their steps! On the base of one which has a sculptured shaft the wall-rue fern was growing. A young starling was perched on the yew by it; he could but just fly, and fluttered across to the sill of the church window. Young birds called pettishly for food from the bushes. Upon the banks hart's-tongue was coming up fresh and green, and the early orchis was in flower. Fern and flower and fledglings had come again as they have come every year since the oldest of these ancient shafts was erected, for life is older, life is greyer, than the weather-beaten mouldings. But life, too, is fresh and young; the stern thought in the stone becomes more cold and grim as the centuries pass away. In the crevices at the foot of another cross wallflowers blossomed, and plants of evening primrose, not yet in flower, were growing. Under a great yew lay the last decaying beam of the stocks. A little yew tree grew on the top of the church tower, its highest branch just above the parapet. A thrush perhaps planted it — thrushes are fond of the viscous yew berries. Through green fields, in which the grass was rising high and sweet, a footpath took me by a solitary mill with an undershot wheel. The sheds about here are often supported on round columns of stone. Beyond the mill is a pleasant meadow, quiet, still and sunlit; buttercup, sorrel and daisy flowered among the grasses down to

the streamlet, where comfrey, with white and pink-lined bells, stood at the water's edge. A renowned painter, Walker, who died early, used to work in this meadow: the original scene from which he took his picture of *The Plough* is not far distant. The painter is gone; the grasses and the flowers are renewed with the summer. As I stood by the brook a water-rat came swimming, drawing a large dock-leaf in his mouth; seeing me, he dived, and took the leaf with him underwater.

Everywhere wild strawberries were flowering on the banks — wild strawberries have been found ripe in January here; everywhere ferns were thickening and extending, foxgloves opening their bells. Another deep coomb led me into the mountainous Quantocks, far below the heather, deep beside another trickling stream. In this land the sound of running water is perpetual, the red flat stones are resonant, and the speed of the stream draws forth music like quick fingers on the keys; the sound of running water and the pleading voice of the willow-wren are always heard in summer. Among the oaks growing on the steep hillside the willow-wrens repeated their sweet prayer; the water as it ran now rose

'Redstarts perched on them' (Mountain Ashes)

and now fell; there was a louder note as a little stone was carried over a fall. The shadow came slowly out from the oak-grown side of the coomb, it reached to the margin of the brook. Under the oaks there appears nothing but red stones, as if the trees were rooted in them; under the boughs probably the grass does not cover the rock as it does on the opposite side. There mountain-ashes flowered in loose order on the green slope. Redstarts perched on them, darting out to seize passing insects. Still deeper in the coomb the oaks stood on either side of the stream; it was the beginning of woods which reach for miles, in which occasionally the wild red deer wander and drink at the clear waters. By now the shadow of the western hilltop had crossed the brooklet, and the still coomb became yet more silent. There was an alder, ivy-grown, beside the stream — a tree with those lines which take an artist's fancy. Under the roots of alders the water-ousel often creeps by day, and the tall heron stalks past at night. Receding up the eastern slope of the coomb the sunlight left the dark alder's foliage in the deep shadow of the hollow. I went up the slope till I could see the sun, and waited; in a few minutes the shadow reached me, and it was sunset; I went still higher, and presently the sun set again. A cool wind was drawing up the coomb, it was dusky in the recesses of the oaks, and the water of the stream had become dark when we emerged from the great hollow, and yet without the summer's evening had but just commenced, and the banks were still heated by the sun.

In contrast to the hills and moors which are so open and wild, the broad vales beneath are closely shut in with hedges. The fields are all of moderate size, unlike the great pastures elsewhere, so that the constant succession of hedges, one after the other, for ten, twenty, or more miles, encloses the country as it were fivefold. Most of the fields are square, or at all events right-angled, unlike the irregular outline and corners of fields in other countries. The number of meadows make it appear as if the land was chiefly grass, though there is really a fair proportion of arable. Over every green hedge there seems a grassy mead; in every hedge trees are numerous, and their thick June foliage, green too, gives a sense of green colour everywhere. But this is relieved with red — the soil is red, and where the plough has been the red furrows stand out so brightly as to seem lifted a little from the level. These red squares when on the side of rising ground show for many miles. The stones are red that lie about, the road dust has a reddish tint, so have the walls of the cottages and mills. Where the banks of the hedges can be seen (or where rabbits have thrown out the earth) they are red, and the water in the ditches and streamlets looks red — it is in fact clear, and the colour is that of the sand and stones. The footpath winds a red band through the grass of the meads, and if it passes under a cliff the rock too rises aslant in red lines. Along the cropped hedges red campions flower so thickly as to take the place of green leaves, and by every gateway red foxgloves grow. Red trifolium is a favourite crop; it is not much redder than the land which bears it. The hues of the red ploughed squares, seen through the trees, vary as the sun dries or the rain moistens the colour. Then, again, the ferns as the summer advances bring forward their green to the aid of the leaves and grass, so that red and green constantly strive together.

There is a fly-rod in every house, almost every felt hat has gut and flies wound round it, and everyone talks trout. Everyone, too, complained that the rivers were so low it was difficult to angle. This circumstance, however, rendered the hues of the rocky banks more distinct. Sitting down to dinner by chance with two farmers, one began to tell me how he had beguiled three trout the previous evening; and the other described how, as he was walking in a field of his by the river, he had seen an otter. These creatures, which are becoming sadly scarce, if not indeed extinct in many counties, are still fairly numerous in the waters here. I hope they will long remain so, for although they certainly do destroy great numbers of fish, yet it must be remembered that in this country our list of wild animals has been gradually decreasing for centuries, and especially wild animals that show sport. The otter, I fear, is going; I hope the sportsmen of Somerset will see that it remains in their county, at all events, when it has become a tradition elsewhere. Otter hounds frequently visit the rivers, and first-rate sport is obtained. In these villages, two hundred miles from London, and often far from the rail, some of the conditions resemble those in the United States, where, instead of shops, 'stores' supply every article from one counter. So here you buy everything in one shop; it is really a 'store' in the American sense. A house which seems amid fields is called 'The Dragon'; you would suppose it an inn, but it is a shop, and has been so ever since the olden times when every trader put out a sign. The sign has gone, but the name remains.

Somewhere in a wood there is a stone, supposed to be a tombstone of the prophetess Mother Shipton, and bearing an undecipherable inscription. One of her rhymes is well remembered in the neighbourhood:-

> When Watchet is all washed down
> Williton shall be a seaport town.

This is founded on the gradual encroachment of the sea, which is a fact, but it will be some time yet before masts are seen at Williton.

At Dunster there is a curious mill which has two wheels, overshot, one in front of the other, and both driven by the same sluice. It was very hot as we stood by the wheels; the mill dust came forth and sprinkled the foliage so that the leaves seemed scarce able to breathe; it drifted almost to the steam hard by, where trout were watching under a cloud of midges

dancing over the ripples. They look as if entangled in an inextricable maze, but if you let your eye travel, say to the right, as you would follow the flight of a bird, you find that one side of the current of insects flies up that way, and the other side returns. They go to and fro in regular order, exactly like the fashionable folk in Rotten Row, but the two ranks pass so quickly that looked at both together the vision cannot separate them, they are faster than the impression on the retina.

At Selworthy a footpath leads up through a wood on Selworthy Hill, and as it ascends, always at the side of the slope, gradually opens out what is perhaps the finest view of Dunkery Beacon, the Dunkery range, and that edge of Exmoor on to the shore of the sea. Across the deep vale the Exmoor mountains rise and reach on either hand, immense breadths of dark heather, deep coombs filled with black shadow, and rounded masses that look dry and heated. To the right is the gleaming sea, and the distant sound of the surge comes up to the wood. The headland and its three curves boldly project into the sunlit waters; from its foot many a gallant stag, hard pressed by the hounds, has swum out into the track of passing vessels. Selworthy Woods were still in the afternoon heat; except for the occasional rustle of a rabbit or of a pheasant, there was no evidence of life; the sound of the sea was faint and soon lost among the ferns. Slowly, very slowly, great Dunkery grew less hard of aspect, shadows drew along at the base, while again the declining sun from time to time sent his beams into valleys till now dark. The thatched house at Holnicote by the foot of Selworthy much interested me; it is one of the last of thatched houses inhabited by a gentleman and landed proprietor. Sir Thomas Acland, who resides here, is a very large owner. Thatch prevails on his estates; thatched cottages, thatched farmhouses, and his thatched mansion. In the coolness of the evening the birds began to sing and squirrels played across the lawn in front of Holnicote House. Bumble-bees hummed in the grass and visited the flowers of the holly bushes. Thrushes sang, and chaffinches, and, sweetest of all, if simplest in notes, the greenfinches talked and courted in the trees. Two cuckoos called in different directions, woodpigeons raised their voices in Selworthy Wood, and rooks went over cawing in their deliberate way. In the level meadow from among the tall grasses and white-flowering wild parsley a landrail called 'crake, crake' ceaselessly. There was a sense of rest and quiet, and with it a joyousness of bird life, such as should be about an English homestead.

English Illustrated Magazine, October 1887

The Water-Colley

THE SWEET grass was wet with dew as I walked through a meadow in Somerset to the river. The cuckoo sang, the pleasanter perhaps because his brief time was nearly over, and all pleasant things seem to have a deeper note as they draw towards an end. Dew and sweet green grass were the more beautiful because of the knowledge that the high hills around were covered by sun-dried, wiry heather. Riverside mead, dew-laden grass, and sparkling stream were like an oasis in the dry desert. They refreshed the heart to look upon as water refreshes the weary. The shadows were more marked and defined than they are as day advances, the hues of the flowers brighter, for the dew was to shadow and flower as if the colours of the artist were not yet dry. Bumble-bees went down with caution into the long grass, not liking to wet their wings. Butterflies and the brilliant moths of a hot summer's morn alight on a dry heated footpath till the dew is gone. A great rock rising from the grass by the river's edge alone looked arid, and its surface already heated, yet it also cast a cool shadow. By a copse, two rabbits — the latest up of all those which had sported during the night — stayed till I came near, and then quietly moved in among the ferns and foxgloves.

In the narrowest part of the wood between the hedge and the river a corncrake called his loudest 'crake, crake', incessantly. The corncrake or landrail is difficult even to see, so closely does he conceal himself in the tall grasses, and his call echoed and re-echoed deceives those who try to find him. Yet by great patience and watchful skilfulness the corncrake is

sometimes caught by hand. If tracked, and if you can see him — the most difficult part — you can put your hand on him. Now and then a corncrake is caught in the same way by hand while sitting on her nest on the ground. It is not, however, as easy as it reads. Walking through the grass, and thinking of the dew and the beautiful morning sunshine, I scarcely noticed the quantity of cuckoo-flowers, or cardamine, till presently it occurred to me that it was very late in the season for cuckoo-flowers; and stooping I picked one, and in the act saw it was an orchis — the early purple. The meadow was coloured, or rather tinted, with the abundance of the orchis, palest of pale, dotted with red, the small narrow leaves sometimes with black spots. They grew in the pasture everywhere, from the river's side in the deep valley to the top of the hill by the wood.

As soon as the surface of the river was in sight I stood and watched, but no ripple or ring of wavelets appeared; the trout were not feeding. The water was so low that the river consisted of a series of pools, connected by rapids descending over ledges of stones and rocky fragments. Illuminated to the very bottom, every trout was visible, even those under the roots of trees and the hollow of the bank. A cast with the fly there was useless; the line would be seen; there was no ripple to hide it. As the trout, too, were in the pools, it might be concluded that those worth

taking had fed, and only the lesser fish would be found in the eddies, where they are permitted by the larger fish to feed after they have finished. Experience and reason were all against the attempt, yet so delightful is the mere motion and delicate touch of the fly-line on the water that I could not but let myself enjoy that at least. The slender lancewood rod swayed, the line swished through the air, and the fly dropped a few inches too high up the rapid among the stones — I had meant it to fall farther across in the dark backwater at the foot of the fall. The swift rush of the current carried the fly instantly downwards, but not so quick as to escape a troutlet; he took it, and was landed immediately. But to destroy these undersized fish was not sport, and as at that moment a water-colley passed I determined to let the trout alone, and observe his ways.

Colley means a blackbird; water-colley, the water-blackbird or water-ousel — called the dipper in the north. In districts where the bird is seldom seen it is occasionally shot and preserved as a white blackbird. But in flight and general appearance the water-colley is almost exactly like a starling with a white neck. His colour is not black or brown — it is a rusty, undecided brown, at a distance something the colour of a young starling, and he flies in a straight line, and yet clumsily, as a young starling does. His very cry, too, sounds immature, pettish, and unfinished, as if from a throat not capable of a full note. There are usually two together, and they pass and re-pass all day as you fish, but if followed are not to be observed without care. I came on the colley too suddenly the first time, at a bend of the river; he was beneath the bank towards me, and flew out from under my feet, so that I did not see him till he was on the wing. Away he flew with a call like a young bird just tumbled out of its nest, following the curves of the stream. Presently I saw him through an alder bush which hid me; he was perched on a root of alder under the opposite bank. Worn away by the stream the dissolved earth had left the roots exposed, the colley was on one of them; in a moment he stepped on to the shore under the hollow, and was hidden behind the roots under a moss-grown stole. When he came out he saw me, and stopped feeding.

He bobbed himself up and down as he perched on the root in the oddest manner, bending his legs so that his body almost touched his perch, and rising again quickly, this repeated in quick succession as if curtsying. This motion with him is a sign of uncertainty — it shows suspicion; after he had bobbed to me ten times off he went. I found him next on a stone in the middle of the river; it stood up above the surface of a rapid connecting two pools. Like the trout, the colley always feeds at the rapids, and flies as they swim, from fall to fall. He was bobbing up and down, his legs bent, and his rusty brown body went up and down, but as I was hidden by a hedge he gained confidence, suspended his curtsying, and began to feed. First he looked all round the stone, and then stepped to another similar island in the midst of the rushing water, pushing his head over the edge into it. Next he stepped into the current, which, though shallow, looked strong enough to sweep him away. The water checked against him rose to the white mark on his breast. He waded up the rapid, every now and then thrusting his head completely under the water; sometimes he was up to his neck, sometimes not so

deep; now and then getting on a stone, searching right and left as he climbed the cascade. The eddying water shot by his slender legs, but he moved against it easily, and soon ascended the waterfall. At the summit a second colley flew past, and he rose and accompanied his friend.

Upon a ledge of rock I saw him once more, but there was no hedge to hide me, and he would not feed; he stood and curtsied, and at the moment of bobbing let his wings too partly down, his tail drooping at the same time. Calling in an injured tone, as if much annoyed, he flew, swept round the meadow, and so to the river behind me. His friend followed. On reaching the river at a safe distance down, he skimmed along the surface like a kingfisher. They find abundance of insect life among the stones at the falls, and everywhere in shallow water. Some accuse them of taking the ova of trout, and they are shot at trout nurseries; but it is doubtful if they are really guilty, nor can they do any appreciable injury in an open stream, not being in sufficient numbers. It is the birds and other creatures peculiar to the water that render fly-fishing so pleasant; were they all destroyed, and nothing left but the mere fish, one might as well stand and fish in a stone cattle-trough. I hope all true lovers of sport will assist in preserving rather than in killing them.

The Manchester Guardian, 31 August 1883

The Makers of Summer

THE LEAVES are starting here and there from green buds on the hedge, but within doors a warm fire is still necessary, when one day there is a slight sound in the room, so peculiar, and yet so long forgotten, that though we know what it is, we have to look at the object before we can name it. It is a house-fly, woke up from his winter sleep, on his way across to the window-pane, where he will buzz feebly for a little while in the sunshire, flourishing best like a hothouse plant under glass. By and by he takes a turn or two under the centrepiece, and finally settles on the ceiling. Then, one or two other little flies of a different species may be seen on the sash; and in a little while the spiders begin to work, and their round silky cocoons are discovered in warm corners of the woodwork. Spiders run about the floors and spin threads by the landing windows; where there are webs it is certain the prey is about, though not perhaps noticed. Next, someone finds a moth. Poor moth! he has to suffer for being found out.

As it grows dusk the bats flitter to and fro by the house; there are moths, then, abroad for them. Upon the cucumber frame in the sunshine perhaps there may be seen an ant or two, almost the first out of the nest; the frame is warm. There are flowers open, despite the cold wind and sunless sky; and as these are fertilised by insects, it follows that there must be more winged, creatures about than we are conscious of. How strange it seems, on a bleak spring day, to see the beautiful pink blossom of the apricot or peach covering the grey wall with colour — snowflakes in the

Nightingale – maker of summer

air at the time! Bright petals are so associated with bright sunshine that this seems backward and inexplicable, till it is remembered that the flower probably opens at the time nearest to that which in its own country brings forth the insects that frequent it. Now and again bumble-bees go by with a burr; and it is curious to see the largest of them all, the big bombus, hanging to the little green gooseberry blossom. Hive-bees, too, are abroad with every stray gleam of sun; and perhaps now and then a drone-fly — last seen on the blossoms of the ivy in November. A yellow butterfly, a white one, afterwards a tortoise-shell — then a sudden pause, and no more butterflies for some time. The rain comes down, and the gay world is blotted out. The wind shifts to the south, and in a few days the first swallows are seen and welcomed, but, as the old proverb says, they do not make a summer. Nor do the long-drawn notes of the nightingale, nor even the jolly cuckoo, nor the tree pipit, no, nor even the soft coo of the turtle-dove and the smell of the mayflower. It is too silent even now: there are the leading notes; but the undertone — the vibration of the organ — is but just beginning. It is the hum of insects and their ceaseless flitting that make the summer more than the birds or the sunshine. The coming of summer is commonly marked in the dates we note by the cuckoo and the swallow and the oak leaves; but till the butterfly and the bee — one with its colour, and one with its hum — fill out the fields, the picture is but an outline sketch. The insects are the details that make the groundwork of a summer day. Till the bumble-bees are working at the clover it is too silent; so I think we may begin our almanack with the house-fly and the moth and the spider and the ant on the cucumber frame, and so on, till finally, the catalogue culminates with the great yellow wasp. He is the final sign of summer; one swallow does not make it, one wasp does. He is a connoisseur of the good things of the earth, and comes not till their season.

On the top of an old wall covered with broad masses of lichen, the patches of which grew out at their edges as if a plate had taken to spreading at its rim, the tits were much occupied in picking out minute insects; the wagtails came too, sparrows, robins, hedge-sparrows, and occasionally a lark; a bare blank wall to all appearance, and the bare lichen as devoid of life to our eyes. Yet there must have been something there for all these eager bills — eggs or pupae. A jackdaw, with iron-grey patch on the back of his broad poll, dropped in my garden one morning, to the great alarm of the small birds, and made off with some large dark object in his beak — some beetle or shell probably, I could not distinguish which, and should most likely have passed the spot without seeing it. The sea-kale, which had been covered up carefully with seaweed, to blanch and to protect it from the frost, was attacked in the cold dry weather in a most furious manner by blackbirds, thrushes and starlings. They tore away the seaweed with their strong bills, pitching it right and left behind them in as workmanlike style as any miner, and so boring deep notches into the edge of the bed. When a blackbird had made a good hole he came back to visit it at various times of the day, and kept a strict watch. If he found any other blackbird or thrush infringing on his diggings, he drove him away ferociously. Never were such works carried on as at the edge of that seaweed; they moved a bushel of it. To the eye there seemed nothing in it but here and there a small white worm; but they found plenty, and the weather being so bitter, I let them do much as they liked; I would rather feed than starve them.

Down at the seashore in the sunny hours, out from the woodwork of the groynes or bulwarks, there came a white spotted spider, which must in some way have known the height to which the tide came at that season, because he was far below the high-water mark. The moles in an upland field had made in the summer a perfect network of runs. Out of curiosity we opened some, and found in them large brown pupae. In the summerhouse, under the wooden eaves, if you look, you will find the chrysalis of a butterfly, curiously slung aslant. Coming down Galley Hill, near Hastings, one day, a party was almost stopped by finding they could only walk on thousands of caterpillars, dark with bright yellow bands, which had sprung out of the grass. The great nettles — now, nothing is so common as a nettle — are sometimes festooned with a dark caterpillar, hundreds upon each plant, hanging like bunches of currants. Could you find a spot the size of your watch-seal without an insect or the germ of one?

Hedge sparrow feeding a cuckoo

The agriculturalists in some southern counties give the boys in spring threepence a dozen for the heads of young birds killed in the nest. The heads are torn off, to be produced, like the wolves' of old times, as evidence of extinction. This — apart from the cruelty of the practice — is, I think, a mistake, for, besides the insects that injure crops, there are some which may be suspected of being inimical to human life, if not directly, indirectly; and if it were not for birds, we should run a very good chance of being literally eaten up. The difficulty is that people cannot believe what they cannot immediately see, and there are very few who have the patience or who feel sufficient interest to study minute things.

I have taken these instances haphazardly; they are large instances, as it were, of big and visible things. They only give the rudest idea of the immensity and complexity of insect life in our own country. My friend the sparrow is, I believe, a friend likewise to man generally. He does a little damage, I admit; but if he were to resort to living on damage solely in his enormous numbers, we should not have a single flower or a single ear of wheat. He does not live by doing mischief alone evidently. He is the best scavenger the Londoners have got, and I counsel them to prize their sparrows, unless they would be overrun with uncomfortable creatures; and possibly he plays his part indirectly in keeping down disease. They say in some places he attacks the crocus. He does not attack mine, so I suspect there must be something wrong with the destroyed crocuses. Some tried to entice him from the flower with crumbs; they would perhaps have succeeded better if they had bought a pint of wheat at the seedsman's and scattered it. In spring, sparrows are not over-fond of crumbs; they are inordinately fond of wheat. During the months of continued dry, cold, easterly winds, which we have had to endure this season, all insect-eating birds have been almost as much starved as they are in winter when there is a deep snow. Nothing comes forth from the ground, nothing from the deep crannies which they cannot peck open; the larva remains quiescent in the solid timber. Not a speck can they find. The sparrow at such a time may therefore be driven to opening flower-buds. Looked at in a broad way, I am convinced he is a friend. I have always let them build about the house, and shall not drive them away.

Peacock butterfly

If you do not know anything of insects, the fields are somewhat barren to you. The buttercups are beautiful, still they are buttercups every day. The thrush's song is lovely, still one cannot always listen to the thrush. The fields are but large open spaces after a time to many, unless they know a little of insects, when at once they become populous, and there is a link found between the birds and the flowers. It is like opening another book of endless pages, and coloured illustrations on every page.

Blessings on the man, said Sancho Panza, who first invented sleep. Blessings on the man who first invented the scarlet geranium, and thereby brought the hummingbird moth to the window-sill; for, though seen ever so often, I can always watch it again hovering over the petals and taking the honey, and away again into the bright sunlight. Sometimes, when walking along, and thinking of everything else but it, the beautiful peacock butterfly suddenly floats by the face like a visitor from another world, so highly coloured, and so original and unlike and unexpected. In bright painters' work like the wings of butterflies, which often have distinct hues side by side, I think nature puts very little green; the bouquet is not backed with maiden-hair fern; the red and the blue and so on have no grass or leaves as a ground colour; nor do they commonly alight on green. The bright colours are left to themselves unrelieved. None of the butterflies, I think, have green on the upper side of the wing; the Green Hairstreak has green under wings, but green is not put forward.

Something the same may be noticed in flowers themselves: the broad surface, for instance, of the peach and apricot, pink without a green leaf; the pear tree white, but the leaves come quickly; the apple, an acre of pink and white, with the merest texture of foliage. Nor are there many conspicuous green insects — the grasshopper; some green flies; the lace-fly, a green body and delicate white wings. With the wild flowers, on the contrary, there seems to come a great deal of green. There is scarcely a colour that cannot be matched in the gay world of wings. Red, blue, yellow, brown and purple — shaded and toned, relieved with dots and curious markings; in the butterflies, night tints in the pattern of the under wings, as if these were shaded with the dusk of the evening, being in shadow under the vane. Gold and orange, red, bright, scarlet, ruby and bronze in the flies. Dark velvet, brown velvet, greys, amber, and gold edgings like military coats in the wild bees. If fifteen or twenty delicate plates of the thinnest possible material, each tinted differently, were placed one over the other, and all translucent, perhaps they might produce something of that singular shadow-painting seen on the wings of moths. They are the shadows of the colours, and yet they are equally distinct. The thin edges of the flies' wings catch the sunbeams, and throw them aside. Look, too, at the bees' limbs, which are sometimes yellow, and sometimes orange-red with pollen. The eyes, too, of many insects are coloured. They know your shadow from that of a cloud. If a cloud comes over, the instant the edge of the shadow reaches the grass moths they stop, so do some of the butterflies and other insects, as the wild bees remain quiescent. As the edge of your shadow falls on them they rise and fly, so that to observe them closely it must not be allowed to overlap them.

Sometimes I think insects smell the approaching observer as the deer wind the stalker. The Gatekeeper butterfly is common; its marking is very ingenious, may I say? regular, and yet irregular. The pattern is complete, and yet it is incomplete; it is finished, and yet it suggests to the mind that the lines ought to go on farther. They go out into space beyond the wing. If a carpet were copied from it, and laid down in a room, the design would want to run through the walls. Imagine the flower-bird's wing detached from some immense unseen carpet and set floating — it is a piece of something not ended in itself, and yet floating about complete. Some of their wings are neatly cut to an edge and bordered; of some the edge is lost in colour, because no line is drawn along it. Some seem to have ragged edges naturally, and look as if they had been battered. Towards the end of their lives little bits of the wing drop out, as if punched. The markings on the under wings have a tendency to run into arches, one arch above the other. The tendency to curve may be traced everywhere in things as wide apart as a flower-bird's wing and the lines on a scallop-shell.

I own to a boyish pleasure in seeing the clouds of brown chafers in early summer clustering on the maple hedges and keeping up a continual burring. They stick to the fingers like the bud of a horse chestnut. Now the fern owl pitches himself over the oaks in the evening as a boy might throw a ball careless whither it goes; the next moment he comes up out of the earth under your feet. The night cuckoo might make another of his many names; his colour, ways, and food are all cuckoo-like; so, too, his immense gape — a cave in which endless moths end their lives; the eggs are laid on the ground, for there is no night-feeding bird into whose nest they could be put, else, perhaps, they would be. There is no night-feeding bird to feed the fern owl's young. Does anyone think the cuckoo could herself feed two young cuckoos? How many birds would it take to feed three young cuckoos? Supposing there were five young cuckoos in the nest, would it not take almost all the birds in a hedge to feed them? For the incredible voracity of the young cuckoo — swallow, swallow, swallow, and gape, gape, gape — cannot be computed. The two robins or the pair of hedge-sparrows in whose nest the young cuckoo is bred, work the day through, and cannot satisfy him; and the mother cuckoo is said to come and assist in feeding him at times. How, then, could the cuckoo feed two or three of its offspring and itself at the same time? Several other birds do not build nests — the plover, the fern owl. That is no evidence of lack of intelligence. The cuckoo's difficulty, or one of its difficulties, seems to be in the providing sufficient food for its ravenous young. A half-fledged cuckoo is already a large bird, and needs a bulk of soft food for its support. Three of them would wear out their mother completely, especially if — as may possibly be the case — the male cuckoo will not help in feeding. This is the simplest explanation, I think; yet, as I have often said before, we must not always judge the ways of birds or animals or insects either by strict utility, or by crediting them with semi-supernatural intelligence. They have their fancies, likes and dislikes, and caprices. There are circumstances — perhaps far back in the life-history of their race — of which we know nothing, but which may influence their conduct unconsciously still, just as the crusades have transmitted a mark to our minds today. Even though an explanation may satisfy us, it is by no means certain that it is the true one, for they may look at matters in an entirely different manner from what we do. The effect of the cuckoo's course is to cause an immense destruction of insects, and it is really one of the most valuable as well as the most welcome of all our birds.

The thin pipe of the gnat heard at night is often alluded to, half in jest, by our older novelists. It is now, I think, dying out a good deal, and local where it stays. It occurred to me, on seeing some such allusion the other day, that it was six years since I had heard a gnat in a bedroom — never since we left a neighbourhood where there had once been marshy ground. Gnats are, however, less common generally — exclusive, of course, of those places where there is much water. All things are local, insects particularly so. On clay soils the flies in summer are most trying; black flies swarm on the eyes and lips, and in the deep lanes cannot be kept off without a green bough. It requires the utmost patience to stay there to observe anything. In a place where the soil was sand, with much heath, on elevated ground, there was no annoyance from flies. There were crowds of them, but they did not attack human beings. You might sit on a bank in the fields with endless insects passing without being irritated; but everywhere out of doors you must listen for the peculiar low whir of the stoat-fly, who will fill his long grey body with your blood in a very few minutes. This is the tsetse of our woods.

Chambers' Journal, 28 May 1887

The Rookery

The Rookery — Building Nests — Young Birds —
Rook Shooting — Stealing Rooks — Antics in the Air
— Mode of Flight — White Rooks

T HE CITY built by the rooks in the elms of the great pasture field
(the Warren, near Wick farmhouse) is divided into two main
parts; the trees standing in two rows, separated by several
hundred yards of sward. But the inhabitants appear to be all more or less
related, for they travel amicably in the same flock and pay the usual visit
to the trees at the same hour. Some scattered elms form a line of
communication between the chief quarters, and each has one or more
nests in it. Besides these, the oaks in the hedgerows surrounding the field
support a few nests, grouped three or four in close neighbourhood. In
some trees near the distant ash-copse there are more nests, whose owners
probably sprang from the same stock, but were exiled, or migrated, and
do not hold much communion with the capital.

In early days men seem to have frequently dug their entrenchments or
planted their stockades on the summit of hills. To the rooks their trees are
their hills, giving security from enemies. The wooden houses in the two
main streets are evidently of greater antiquity than those erected in the
outlying settlements. The latter are not large or thick: they are clearly the
work of one, or at most two, seasons only; for it is noticeable that when
rooks build at a distance from the centre of population they are some time
before they finally decide on a site, abandoning one place after another.
But the nests forming the principal streets are piled up to a considerable
height — fresh twigs being added every year — and are also thick and
bulky. The weight of the whole must be a heavy burden to the trees.

Much skill is shown in the selection of the branches upon which the foundations are laid. In the first place, the branch must fork sufficiently to hold the bottom twigs firmly and to give some side-support. Then it must be a branch more or less vertical, or it would swing with the wind too much up and down as well as to and fro. Thirdly, there should be a clear or nearly clear space above the nest to give easy access, and to afford room for it to increase in size annually. For this reason, perhaps, nests are generally placed near the top or outer sides of the tree, where the boughs are smaller, and every upward extension reaches a clearer place. Fourthly, the bough ought not to be too stiff and firm; it should yield a little, and sway easily, though only in a small degree, to the breeze. If too stiff, in strong gales the nest runs the risk of being blown clean out of the tree. Fifthly, no other branch must rub against the one bearing the principal weight of the nest, for that would loosen the twigs in time, and dislocate the entire structure. Finally, rooks like an adjacent bough on which the bird not actually engaged in incubation can perch and 'caw' to his mate, and which is also useful to alight on when bringing food for the young.

It may be that the difficulty of finding trees which afford all these necessary conditions is one reason why rooks who settle at a distance from their city seem long before they can please themselves. The ingenuity exercised in the selection of the bough and in the placing of the twigs is certainly very remarkable. When the wind blows furiously you may see the nest moving gently, riding on the swaying boughs, while one of the birds perches on the branch close by, and goes up and down like a boat on the waves. Except by the concussion of branches beating hard against the nest, it is rarely broken; up to a certain point it would seem as if the older nests are the firmest, perhaps because of their weight. Sometimes one which has been blown down in the winter — when the absence of protecting leaves gives the wind more power on them — retains its general form even after striking against branches in its descent and after collision with the earth.

Elms are their favourite trees for building in. Oak and ash are also used, but where there are sufficient elms they seem generally preferred. These trees, as a rule, grow higher than any others ordinarily found in the fields, and are more frequently seen in groups, rows, or avenues, thus giving the rook facilities for placing a number of nests in close neighbourhood. The height of the elm affords greater safety, and the branches are perhaps better suited for their purpose.

After building in an elm for many years — perhaps ever since the owner can remember — rooks will suddenly desert it. There are the old nests still; but no effort is made to repair them, and no new ones are made. The winds and storms presently loosen the framework, over which no care is now taken, and portions are blown down. Then by and by the discovery is made that the tree is rapidly dying. The leaves do not appear, or if they do they wither and turn yellow before midsummer: gradually the branches decay and fall of their own weight or before the wind.

No doubt if anyone had carefully examined the tree he would have observed signs of decay long before the rooks abandoned it; but those who pass the same trees day after day for years do not observe minute changes, or, if they do, as nature is slow in her movements, get so accustomed to the sight of the fungi about the base, and the opening

bark where the decomposing touchwood shows, as to think that it will always be so. At last the rooks desert it, and then the truth is apparent.

Their nests, being heavy, are not safe on branches up which the strengthening sap no longer rises; and in addition to the nest there is the weight of the sitting-bird, and often that of the other who perches temporarily on the edge. As the branches die they become stiff, and will not bend to the gale; this immobility is also dangerous to the nest. So long as the bough yields and sways gently — not much, but still a little — the strong winds do no injury. When the bough becomes rigid, the broad side or wall of the nest offers an unyielding surface, which is accordingly blown away.

The nests which contain young are easily distinguished, despite the height, by the almost continuous cry for food. The labour of feeding the voracious creatures must be immense, and necessity may partly account for the greater boldness of the old birds at that season. By counting the nests from which the cry proceeds the condition of the rookery is ascertained, and the amount of sport it will afford reckoned with some certainty. By noting the nests from which the cry arose last, it is known which trees to avoid in the rook-shooting; for the young do not all come to maturity at the same time, and there are generally a dozen or so which it is best to leave a week or a fortnight later than the rest.

When the young birds begin to quit the nests, and are observed perching on the tree or fluttering from branch to branch, they must not be left much longer before shooting, or they will wander and be lost. A very few days will then make all the difference; and so it has often happened that men expecting to make a great bag have been quite disappointed, notwithstanding the evident number of nests; the shooting has been held a day or so too late. The young birds get the use of their wings very quickly, and their instinct rather seems to be to wander than to remain in the immediate vicinity of their birthplace.

Some think that the old birds endeavour to entice them away as much as possible, knowing what is coming. It may be doubted if that is the case with respect to the very young birds; but when the young ones are capable of something like extended flight, and can cross a field without much difficulty, I think the parents do attempt to lead them away. When the shooting is in progress, if you will go a little distance from the rookery, out of the excitement of the sport, you may sometimes see two old rooks, one on each side of a young one, cawing to it with all their might. The young bird is, perhaps, on the ground, or on a low hedge, and the old birds are evidently endeavouring to get it to move. Yet they have not learned the only way in which that can be done — i.e. by starting themselves and flying a short distance, and waiting, when the young bird will almost invariably follow.

If you approach the trio the two old birds at once take flight, seeing your gun, and the young bird in a few seconds goes after them. Had they the sense to repeat this operation, they might often draw the young one away from danger; as for their cawing, it does not seem to be quite understood by their offspring, who have hardly yet learned their own language.

To appreciate this effort on the part of the old birds, it must be recollected that immediately after the first shot the great mass of the old rooks fly off in alarm. They go to some distance and then wheel round and come back at an immense height, and there, collected in loose order, circle round and round, cawing as they sail. For an old rook to remain in or near the rookery when once the firing has commenced is the exception, and must be a wonderful effort of moral courage, for of all birds rooks seem most afraid of a gun; and naturally so, having undergone, when themselves young, a baptism of fire. Those that escape slaughter are for the most part early birds that come to maturity before the majority, and so leave the trees before the date fixed for shooting arrived, or acquire a power of flight sufficient to follow their parents on the first alarm to a safe distance. They have, therefore, a good opportunity of witnessing the destruction of their cousins, and do not forget the lesson.

Although the young birds upon getting out of the nest under ordinary conditions seem to like to wander, yet if they are driven out or startled by the shot they do not then at once endeavour to make for the open country or to spread abroad, but appear rather to cling to the place, as if the old nests could shelter them. After a while they begin to understand the danger of this proceeding, and half an hour's rapid firing causes the birds to spread about and get into the trees in the hedges at some distance. There of course they are pursued, or killed the next day, three-quarters of a mile or more away from home. It is rare for old rooks to get shot, for the reason above stated: they rise into the air out of reach. Those that are killed are generally such as have lingered in the hope to save a young bird, and are mistaken and shot as young themselves.

Young birds may be easily distinguished by their slow uncertain flight and general appearance of not knowing exactly where to go or what to do. They are especially easy to pick out if you see them about to perch on a tree. They go at the tree anyhow, crash in among the branches, and rather fall on a perch than choose it. The old bird always enters a tree carefully, as if he did not like to ruffle his feathers, and knew precisely what sort of bough he preferred to settle on. Close to the rookery there is no need to wait to pick out the young birds, because they are all sure to be young birds there; but, as observed, old birds will linger with young ones at a little distance, and may then be mistaken — as also on the following day, when sportsmen go round to pick up the outsiders, and frequently come on old and young together. The old bird will not sit and let you aim at him perching; if you shoot him, it must be on the wing. The young bird will sit and let you pick him off with a crossbow, and even if a cartridge singes his wing he will sometimes only hop a yard or two along the boughs.

Though hard hit and shattered with shot, they will cling to the branches convulsively, seeming to hang by the crook of the claw or by muscular contraction even when perfectly dead, till lifted up by a shot fired directly underneath, or till the bough itself is skilfully cut off by a cartridge and both come down together. The young feathers being soft, and the quills not so hard as in older birds, scarcely a rook-shooting ever goes by without someone claiming to have made a tremendous long shot, which is quite possible, as it does not require many pellets or much force behind them.

On dropping a rook, probably at some distance from the rookery, where the men are whose duty it is to collect the slain, beware of carrying the bird; let him die, or at most throw him upon a bramble bush in a conspicuous spot till a boy comes round. Rooks are perfectly infested with vermin, which in a few minutes will pass up their legs on to your hand, and cause an unpleasant irritation, though it is only temporary — for the insects cannot exist long away from the bird.

The young birds are occasionally stolen from the nests, notwithstanding the difficulty of access. Young labourers will climb the trees, though so large that they can scarcely grasp the trunk, and with few branches, and those small for some height; for elms are often stripped up the trunk to make the timber grow straight and free from the great branches called 'limbs'. Even when the marauder is in the tree he has some difficulty in getting at the nests, which are placed where the boughs diminish in size. Climbing-irons used to be sometimes employed for the purpose. As elm trees are so conspicuous, these thieving practices cannot well be carried on while it is light. So the rook-poachers go up the trees in the dead of night; and as the old rooks would make a tremendous noise

and so attract attention, they carry a lantern with them, the light from which silences the birds. So long as they can see a light they will not caw.

The time selected to rob a rookery is generally just before the date fixed for shooting, because the young birds are of little use for cooking till ready to fly. The trick, it is believed, has often been played, for the mere pleasure of spiting the owner, the very night previous to the rook-shooting party being chosen. These robberies of young rooks are much less frequent than they used to be. One reason why those who possess any property in the country do not like to see a labouring man with a gun is because he will shoot an old rook (and often eat it) if he gets the opportunity, without reference to times or seasons, whether they are building or not.

The young rooks that escape being shot seem to be fed, or partly fed, by the old birds for some time after they can fly well and follow their parents. It is easy to know when there are young rooks in a flock feeding in a field. At the first glance the rooks look scattered about, without any order, each independent of the other. But in a few minutes it will be noticed that here and there are groups of three, which keep close together. These are formed of the parents and the young bird — apparently as big and as black as themselves — which they feed now and then. The young bird, by attending to their motions, learns where to find the best food. As late as July trios like this may sometimes be seen.

Besides the young birds that have the good fortune to pass unscathed through the dangers of rook-shooting day, and escape being knocked over afterwards, some few get off on account of having been born earlier than the majority, thus possessing a stronger power of flight. Some nests are known to be more forward than the others; but although the young birds may be on the point of departing, they are not killed because the noise of the firing would disturb the whole settlement. So that it becomes the rook's interest to incubate a little in advance of the rest.

After a few months they are put into another terrible fright — on the 1st of September. Guns are going off in all directions, no matter where they turn, so that they find it impossible to feel at ease, and instead of feeding wheel about in the air, or settle on the trees.

The glossy plumage of the rook will sometimes, when seen at a certain angle, reflect the sun's rays in such a manner that instead of looking black the bird appears clothed in shining light: it is as if the feathers were polished like a mirror. In feeding they work in a grave, steady way — a contrast to the restless starlings who so often accompany them. They do not put a sentinel in a tree to give warning of the approach of an enemy. The whole flock is generally on the ground together, and if half a dozen perch awhile on the trees, they soon descend. So far are they from setting a watch, that if you pass up outside the hedge to the leeward, on any side except where the wind would carry the noise of footsteps to them, it is easy to get close — sometimes, if they are feeding near the hedge, within three or four yards. Of course, if a rook happens to be in a tree it will not be possible to do so; but they do not set a sentinel for this purpose.

Rooks, in a general way, seem more at their ease in the meadows than in the arable fields. In the latter they are constantly fired at, if only with blank charges, to alarm them from the seed, besides being shouted at and frightened with clappers. The birdkeeper's efforts are, however, of very little avail. If he puts the flock up on one side of the field, they lazily sail to a distant corner, and when he gets there go back again. They are fully aware that he cannot injure them if they keep a certain distance; but this perpetual driving to and fro makes them suspicious. In the meadows it is rare for them to be shot at, and they are consequently much less timid.

At the same time they can perfectly well distinguish a gun from a walking-stick. If you enter a meadow with a gun under your arm, and find a flock feeding, they immediately cease searching for food and keep a strict watch on your movements; and if you approach they are off directly. If you carry a walking-stick only, you may pass within thirty yards sometimes, and they take little notice, provided you use the stick in the proper way. But now lift it, and point it at the nearest rook, and in an instant he is up with a 'caw' of alarm — though he knows it is not a gun — and flies just above the surface of the ground till he considers himself safe from possibility of danger. Often the whole flock will move before that gesture. It is noticeable that no wild creatures, birds or animals, like anything pointed at them; you may swing your stick freely, but point it, and off goes the finch that showed no previous alarm. So, too, dogs do not seem easy if a stick is pointed at them.

Rooks are easily approached in the autumn, when gorging the acorns. They may often be seen flying carrying an acorn in the bill. Sometimes a flock will set to work and tear up the grass by the roots over a wide space — perhaps nearly half an acre — in search of a favourite beetle. The grass is pulled up in little wisps, just about as much as they can hold in their beaks at a time. In spring they make tracks through the mowing-grass — not in all the meadows, but only in one here and there, where they find the food they prefer. These tracks are very numerous, and do the grass some damage. Besides following the furrows made by the plough, and destroying grubs, beetles, wireworm and other pests in incalculable numbers, they seem to find a quantity of insect food in unripe corn; for they often frequent wheatfields only just turning yellow, and where the grain is not yet developed. Except perhaps where they are very numerous, they do much more good than harm.

Rooks may now and then be seen in the autumn, on the hayricks; they pull the thatch out, and will do in this way an injury to the roof. Therefore old black bottles are often placed on the thatch in order to scare them. It is said that they pull out the straw for the stray grains left in the ear by the threshing-machine. This seems doubtful. It appears more probable that some insect found on the straw attracts them.

If you are walking past a feeding flock, the nearest rook to you will often exhibit a ridiculous indecision as to whether he shall fly or not. He stretches his neck and leans forward as if about to spring, stops, utters a questioning 'Cawk?' then watches you a moment and gives a hop, just opens his wings, shuts them, and descends within a couple of feet. 'Cawk!' again. Finally, if you turn from your course and make a step towards him, he rises, flaps his wings three or four times, extends them, and glides a dozen yards to alight once more.

Sometimes a flock will rise in the air, and silently wheel round and round after each other, gradually ascending and drifting slowly with the current till they reach a great height. When they soar like this it is said to foretell fine weather. At another time a flock will go up and wheel about in the strangest irregular manner. Every now and then one will extend his wings, holding them rigid, and dive downwards, in his headlong descent wavering to and fro like a sheet of paper falling edge first. He falls at a great pace, and looks as if he must be dashed to pieces against a tree or the earth; but he rights himself at the last moment, and glides away and up again with ease. Occasionally two or three rooks may be seen doing this at once, while the rest whirl about as if possessed; and those that are diving utter a gurgling sound like the usual cawk prolonged — 'caw-wouk.' These antics are believed to foretell rough winds.

The rook, like other broad-winged birds, often makes much leeway in flying, though there be only a moderate wind. The beak points in one direction, in which the bird is apparently proceeding, but if observed closely it will be found that the real course is somewhat sideways. He is making leeway. So it is that a rook which looks as if coming straight towards you — as if he must inevitably go overhead — passes some distance to one side. He appears slow on the wing, as if to go fast required more energy than he possessed, yet he travels over great distances without the lease apparent exertion.

When going with the wind he sails high in the air, only flapping his wings sufficiently to maintain balance and steering power. But when working against the wind, if it is a strong gale, his wings are used rapidly, and he comes down near the surface of the ground. He then flies just above the grass, only high enough to escape touching it, and follows the contour of the field. At the hedges he has to rise, and immediately meets the full force of the breeze. It is so powerful sometimes that he cannot overcome it, and his efforts simply lift him in the air, like a kite drawn against the wind. For a few moments he appears stationary, his own impetus and the contending wind balancing each other, and holding him suspended. Then he rises again, but still finding the current too strong, tacks like a ship to port or starboard, and so works aslant into the gale. Shortly afterwards he comes down again, if the field be a large one, and glides forward in the same manner as before, close to the surface. In crossing the lake, too, against the wind, he flies within a few feet of the water.

During such a gale a rook may often be seen struggling to get over a row of trees, and stationary, though using his wings vigorously, suspended a little way above the topmost branches. Frequently he has to give up the attempt, turn back, and make a detour.

Though rooks usually go in flocks, individuals sometimes get separated, and may be seen flying alone on the way to rejoin their friends. A flock of rooks, on rising, occasionally divides into two or more parties. Each section wheels off on its own course, while sometimes a small number of those who chance to be near the centre of the original formation seem at a loss which company to follow, and settle down again on the field. So a dozen or more become separated from the crowd, and presently, when they rise, they too divide; three or four fly one way to join one section, and others take another route. Individuals thus find themselves alone; but that causes them no uneasiness, as they have their well-known places of rendezvous, and have only to fly to certain fields to be sure of meeting their friends, or at most to wait about near the nesting-trees till the rest come.

It must not, therefore, be supposed that every one flying alone is a crow. Crows are scarce in comparison with rooks. In severe weather a rook will sometimes venture into the courtyard of the farmstead.

Two rooks marked with white resided at the rookery here for several years. One had sufficient white to be distinguished at a distance; the other seemed to have but one or two feathers, which were, however, visible enough when near the bird. As they have not been seen lately, they have probably been shot by some one who thought it clever to destroy anything out of the ordinary. Most large rookeries can either show a rook with white feathers, or have well-authenticated records of their former existence; but though not rare, people naturally like to preserve them when they do occur, and it is extremely annoying to have them wantonly killed.

Pall Mall Gazette, 25 & 30 September 1878

The Acorn-Gatherer

BLACK ROOKS, yellow oak leaves, and a boy asleep at the foot of the tree. His head was lying on a bulging root close to the stem: his feet reached to a small sack or bag half full of acorns. In his slumber his forehead frowned — they were fixed lines, like the grooves in the old bark. There was nothing else in his features attractive or repellent: they were such as might have belonged to a dozen hedge children. The set angry frown was the only distinguishing mark — like the dents on a penny made by a hobnail boot, by which it can be known from twenty otherwise precisely similar. His clothes were little better than sacking, but clean, tidy, and repaired. Anyone would have said, 'Poor, but carefully tended.' A kind heart might have put a threepenny-bit in his clenched little fist, and sighed. But that iron set frown on the young brow would not have unbent even for the silver. Caw! Caw!

The happiest creatures in the world are the rooks at the acorns. It is not only the eating of them, but the finding: the fluttering up there and hopping from branch to branch, the sidling out to the extreme end of the bough, and the inward chuckling when a friend lets his acorn drop tip-tap from bough to bough. Amid such plenty they cannot quarrel or fight, having no cause of battle, but they can boast of success, and do so to the loudest of their voices. He who has selected a choice one flies with it as if it were a nugget in his beak, out to some open spot of ground, followed by a general Caw!

This was going on above while the boy slept below. A thrush looked out from the hedge, and among the short grass there was still the hum of bees, constant sun-worshippers as they are. The sunshine gleamed on the rooks' black feathers overhead, and on the sward sparkled from hawkweed, some lotus and yellow weed, as from a faint ripple of water. The oak was near a corner formed by two hedges, and in the angle was a narrow thorny gap. Presently an old woman, very upright, came through this gap carrying a faggot on her shoulder and a stout ash stick in her hand. She was very clean, well dressed for a labouring woman, hard of feature, but superior in some scarcely defined way to most of her class. The upright carriage had something to do with it, the firm mouth, the light blue eyes that looked everyone straight in the face. Possibly these, however, had less effect than her conscious righteousness. Her religion lifted her above the rest, and I do assure you that it was perfectly genuine. That hard face and cotton gown would have gone to the stake.

When she had got through the gap she put the faggot down in it, walked a short distance out into the field, and came back towards the boy, keeping him between her and the corner. Caw! said the rooks, Caw! Caw! Thwack, thwack, bang, went the ash stick on the sleeping boy, heavily enough to have broken his bones. Like a piece of machinery suddenly let loose, without a second of dubious awakening and without a cry, he darted straight for the gap in the corner. There the faggot stopped him, and before he could tear it away the old woman had him again, thwack, thwack, and one last stinging slash across his legs as he doubled past her. Quick as the wind as he rushed he picked up the bag of acorns and pitched it into the mound, where the acorns rolled down into a pond and were lost — a good round shilling's worth. Then across the field, without his cap, over the rising ground, and out of sight. The old woman made no attempt to hold him, knowing from previous experience that it was useless, and would probably result in her own overthrow. The faggot, brought a quarter of a mile for the purpose, enabled her, you see, to get two good chances at him.

A wickeder boy never lived: nothing could be done with the reprobate. He was her grandson — at least, the son of her daughter, for he was not legitimate. The man drunk, the girl died, as was believed, of sheer starvation: the granny kept the child, and he was now between ten and eleven years old. She had done and did her duty, as she understood it. A prayer-meeting was held in her cottage twice a week, she prayed herself aloud among them, she was a leading member of the sect. Neither example, precept nor the rod could change that boy's heart. In time perhaps she got to beat him from habit rather than from any particular anger of the moment, just as she fetched water and filled her kettle, as one of the ordinary events of the day. Why did not the father interfere? Because if so he would have had to keep his son: so many shillings a week the less for ale.

In the garden attached to the cottage there was a small shed with a padlock, used to store produce or wood in. One morning, after a severe beating, she drove the boy in there and locked him in the whole day without food. It was no use, he was as hardened as ever.

A footpath which crossed the field went by the cottage, and every Sunday those who were walking to church could see the boy in the window with granny's Bible open before him. There he had to sit, the door locked, under terror of stick, and study the page. What was the use of compelling him to do that? He could not read. 'No,' said the old woman, 'he won't read, but I makes him look at his book.'

The thwacking went on for some time, when one day the boy was sent on an errand two or three miles, and for a wonder started willingly enough. At night he did not return, nor the next day, nor the next, and it was as clear as possible that he had run away. No-one thought of tracking his footsteps, or following up the path he had to take, which passed a railway, brooks and a canal. He had run away, and he might stop away: it was beautiful summer weather, and it would do him no harm to stop out for a week. A dealer who had business in a field by the canal thought indeed that he saw something in the water, but he did not want any trouble, nor indeed did he know that someone was missing. Most likely a dead dog; so he turned his back and went to look again at the cow he thought of buying. A barge came by, and the steerswoman, with a pipe in her mouth, saw something roll over and come up under the rudder: the length of the barge having passed over it. She knew what it was, but she wanted to reach the wharf and go ashore and have a quart of ale. No use picking it up, only makes a mess on deck, there was no reward — 'Gee-up! Neddy.' The barge went on, turning up the mud in the shallow water, sending ripples washing up to the grassy meadow shores, while the moorhens hid in the flags till it was gone. In time a labourer walking on the towing-path saw 'it,' and fished it out, and with it a slender ash sapling, with twine and hook, a worm still on it. This was why the dead boy had gone so willingly, thinking to fish in the 'river', as he called the canal. When his feet slipped and he fell in, his fishing-line somehow became twisted about his arms and legs, else most likely he would have scrambled out, as it was not very deep. This was the end; nor was he even remembered. Does anyone sorrow for the rook, shot, and hung up as a scarecrow? The boy had been talked to, and held up as a scarecrow all his life: he was dead, and that is all. As for granny, she felt no twinge: she had done her duty.

Longman's Magazine, vol. 1, no. v, pp. 515-524, March 1883

This version from *Bits of Oak Bark*, part 1, March 1883

An English Deerpark

THERE IS an old park wall which follows the highway in all its
turns with such fidelity of curve that for some two miles it seems
as if the road had been fitted to the wall. Against it hawthorn
bushes have grown up at intervals, and in the course of years their trunks
have become almost timber. Ivy has risen round some of these and,
connecting them with the wall, gives them at a distance the appearance
of green bastions. Large stems of ivy, too, have flattened themselves upon
the wall, as if with arched back they were striving like athletes to
overthrow it. Mosses, brown, in summer, soft green in winter, cover it
where there is shadow, and if pulled up take with them some of the
substance of the stone or mortar like a crust. A dry, dusty fern may
perhaps be found now and then on the low bank at the foot — a fern
that would rather be within the park than thus open to the heated south
with the wall reflecting the sunshine behind. On the other side of the
road, over the thin hedge, there is a broad plain of cornfields. Coming
from these the labourers have found out, or made, notches in the wall; so
that, by putting the iron-plated toes of their boots in, and holding to the
ivy, they can scale it and shorten their long trudge home to the village. In
the spring the larks, passing from the green corn to the pasture within,
fluttering over with gently vibrating wings and singing as they daintily
go, sometimes settle on the top. There too the yellowhammers stay. In
the crevices blue tits build deep inside passages that abruptly turn, and
baffle egg-stealers. Partridges come over with a whirr, but just clearing the

top, gliding on extended wings, which to the eye look like a slight brown crescent. The waggoners who go by know that the great hawthorn bastions are favourite resorts of woodpigeons and missel-thrushes. The haws are ripe in autumn and the ivy berries in spring, so that the bastions yield a double crop. A mallow, the mauve petals of which even the dust of the road cannot impair, flowers here and there on the dry bank below, and broad moon-daisies among the ripe and almost sapless grass of midsummer.

If anyone climbed the wall from the park and looked across at the plain of cornfields in early spring, everywhere there would be seen brown dots in the air — above the first slender green blades; above the freshly turned dark furrows; above the distant plough, the share of which, polished like a silver mirror by friction with the clods, reflects the sunshine, flashing a heliograph message of plenty from the earth; everywhere brown dots, and each a breathing creature — larks ceaselessly singing, and all unable to set forth their joy. Swift is the vibration of their throats, they cannot pour the notes fast enough to express their eager welcome. As a shower falls from the sky, so falls the song of the larks. There is no end to them: they are everywhere; over every acre away across the plain to the downs, and up on the highest hill. Every crust of English bread has been sung over at its birth in the green blade by a lark.

If one looked again in June, the clover itself, a treasure of beauty and sweetness, would be out, and the south wind would come over acres of flower — acres of clover, beans, tares, purple trifolium, far-away crimson sainfoin (brightest of all on the hills), scarlet poppies, pink convolvulus, yellow charlock, and green wheat coming into ear. In August, already squares would be cut into the wheat, and the sheaves rising, bound about the middle, hour-glass fashion; some breadths of wheat yellow, some golden-bronze; besides these, white barley and oats, and beans blackening. Turtle-doves would be in the stubble, for they love to be near the sheaves. The hills after or during rain look green and near; on sunny days, a far and faint blue. Sometimes the sunset is caught in the haze on them and lingers, like a purple veil about the ridges. In the dusk hares come heedlessly along; the elder-bushes gleam white with creamy petals through the night.

Sparrows and partridges alike dust themselves in the white dust, an inch deep, of midsummer, in the road between the wall and the corn — a pitiless Sahara road to traverse at noonday in July, when the air is still and you walk in a hollow way, the yellow wheat on one side and the wall on the other. There is shade in the park within, but a furnace of sunlight without — weariness to the eyes and feet from glare and dust. The wall winds with the highway and cannot be escaped. It goes up the slight elevations and down the slopes; it has become settled down and bound with time. But presently there is a steeper dip, and at the bottom, in a narrow valley, a streamlet flows out from the wheat into the park. A spring rises at the foot of the down a mile away, and the channel it has formed winds across the plain. It is narrow and shallow; nothing but a larger furrow, filled in winter by the rains rushing off the fields, and in summer a rill scarce half-an-inch deep. The wheat hides the channel completely, and as the wind blows, the tall ears bend over it. At the edge of the bank pink convolvulus twines round the stalks and the green-flowered buckwheat gathers several together. The sunlight cannot reach the stream, which runs in shadow, deep down below the wheatears, over which butterflies wander. Forget-me-nots flower under the banks; grasses lean on the surface; willow-herbs, tall and stiff, stand up; but out from the tangled and interlaced fibres the water flows as clear as it rose by the hill. There is a culvert under the road, and on the opposite side the wall admits the stream by an arch jealously guarded by bars. In this valley the wall is lower and thicker and less covered at the top with ivy, so that where the road rises over the culvert you can see into the park. The stream goes rounding away through the sward, bending somewhat to the right, where the ground gradually descends. On the left side, at some distance, stands a row of full-grown limes, and through these there is a glimpse of the old manor-house. It is called the old house because the requirements of modern days have rendered it unsuitable for an establishment. A much larger mansion has been erected in another part of the park nearer the village, with a façade visible from the highway. The old manor-house is occupied by the land-steward, or, as he prefers to be called, the deputy-forester, who is also the oldest and largest tenant on the estate. It is he who rules the park. The labourers and keepers call him the 'squire'.

Now the old squire's favourite resort is the window-seat in the gun-room, because thence he can see a section of the highway, which, where it crosses the streamlet, comes within half a mile of the house. There the hollow and the lower wall permit anyone at this window to obtain a view of the road on one of the sides of the valley. At this declivity it almost faces the house, and whether the passers-by are going to the market town, or returning to the village, they cannot escape observation. If they come from the town, the steep descent compels them to walk their horses down it; if from the village, they have a hard pull up. So the oaken window-seat in the gun-room is as polished and smooth as an old saddle; for if the squire is indoors, he is certain to be there. He often rests there after half-an-hour's work on one or other of the guns in the rack; for, though he seldom uses but one, he likes to take the locks to pieces upon a little bench which he has fitted up, and where he has a vice, tools, a cartridge-loading apparatus, and so forth, from which the room acquired its name. With the naked eye, however, as the road is half-a-mile distant, it is not possible to distinguish persons, except in cases of very pronounced individuality. Nevertheless old 'Ettles', the keeper, always declared that he could see a hare run up the down from the park, say a mile and a half. This may be true; but in the gun-room there is a field-glass, said to have been used at the seige of Seringapatam, which the squire can bring to bear upon the road in an instant, for from constant use at the same focus there is a rim round the tarnished brass. No time, therefore, need be lost in trials; it can be drawn out to the well-known mark at once. The window itself is large, but there is a casement in it — a lesser window — which can be thrown open with a mere twist of the thumb on the button, and as it swings open it catches itself on a hasp. Then the field-glass examines the distant wayfarer.

When people have dwelt for generations in one place they come to know the history of their immediate world. There was not a waggon that went by without a meaning to the squire. One perhaps brought a load of wool from the downs; it was old Hobbes's, whose affairs he had known these forty years. Another, with wheat, was Lambourne's team: he lost heavily in 1879, the wet year. The family and business concerns of every man of any substance were as well known to the squire as if they had been written in a chronicle. So, too, he knew the family tendency, as it were, of the cottagers. So-and-so's lads were always tall, another's girls always tidy. If you employed a member of this family, you were sure to be well served; if of another, you were sure to be cheated in some way. Men vary like trees: an ash sapling is always straight, the bough of an oak

crooked, a fir full of knots. A man, said the squire, should be straight like a gun. This section of the highway gave him the daily news of the village as the daily papers gave us the news of the world. About two hundred yards from the window the row of limes began, each tree as tall and large as an elm, having grown to its full natural size. The last of the row came very near obstructing the squire's line of sight, and it once chanced that some projecting branches by degrees stretched out across his field of view. This circumstance caused him much mental trouble; for, having all his life consistently opposed any thinning out or trimming of trees, he did not care to issue an order which would almost confess a mistake. Besides which, why only these particular branches? — the object would be so apparent. The squire, directed his steps beneath these limes, and, striking the offending boughs with his stick, remarked that they grew extremely fast. But the keeper, usually so keen to take a hint, only answered that the lime was the quickest wood to grow of which he knew. In his heart he enjoyed the squire's difficulty. Finally the squire, legalising his foible by recognising it, fetched a ladder and a hatchet, and chopped off the boughs with his own hands.

It was from the gun-room window that the squire observed the change of the seasons and the flow of time. The larger view he often had on horseback of miles of country did not bring it home to him. The old familiar trees, the sward, the birds, these told him of the advancing or receding sun. As he reclined in the corner of the broad window-seat, his feet up, and drowsy, of a summer afternoon, he heard the languid cawing of an occasional rook, for rooks are idle in the heated hours of the day. He was aware, without conscious observation, of the swift, straight line drawn across the sky by a woodpigeon. The pigeons were continually to and fro the cornfields outside the wall to the south and the woods to the north, and their shortest route passed directly over the limes. To the limes the bees went when their pale yellow flowers appeared. Not many butterflies floated over the short sward, which was fed too close for flowers. The butterflies went to the old garden, rising over the high wall as if they knew beforehand of the flowers that were within. Under the sun the short grass dried as it stood, and with the sap went its green.

There came a golden tint on that part of the wheatfields which could be seen over the road. A few more days — how few they seemed! — and there was a spot of orange on the beech in a little copse near the limes. The bucks were bellowing in the forest: as the leaves turned colour their loves began and the battles for the fair. Again a few days and the snow came, and rendered visible the slope of the ground in the copse between the trunks of the trees: the ground there was at other times indistinct under brambles and withered fern. The squire left the window for his armchair by the fire; but if presently, as often happens when frost quickly follows a snowstorm, the sun shone out and a beam fell on the wall, he would get up and look out. Every footstep in the snow contained a shadow cast by the side, and the dazzling white above and the dark within produced a blue tint. Yonder by the limes the rabbits ventured out for a stray bunch of grass not quite covered by the drift, tired, no doubt, of the bitter bark of the ash-rods that they had nibbled in the night. As they scampered, each threw up a white cloud of snowdust behind him. Yet a few days and the sward grew greener. The pale winter hue, departing as the spring mist came trailing over, caught for a while in the copse, and, lingering there, the ruddy buds and twigs of the limes were refreshed. The larks rose a little way to sing in the moist air. A rook, too, perching on the top of a low tree, attempted other notes than his monotonous caw. So absorbed was he in his song that you might have walked under him unnoticed. He uttered four or five distinct sounds that would have formed a chant, but he paused between each as if uncertain of his throat. Then, as the sun shone, with a long-drawn 'ca-awk' he flew to find his mate, for it would soon be time to repair the nest in the limes. The butterflies came again and the year was completed, yet it seemed but a few days to the squire. Perhaps if he lived for a thousand years, after a while he would wonder at the rapidity with which the centuries slipped by.

By the limes there was a hollow — a little circular copse was on the slope — and jays came to it as they worked from tree to tree across the park. Their screeching often echoed through the open casement of the gun-room. A faint mark on the sward trended towards this hollow; it was

a trail made by the squire, one of whose favourite strolls was in this direction. This summer morning, taking his gun, he followed the trail once more.

The grass was longer and coarser under the shadow of the limes, and upborne on the branches were numerous little sticks which had dropped from the rookery above. Sometimes there was an overthrown nest like a sack of twigs turned out on the turf, such as the hedgers rake together after faggoting. Looking up into the trees on a summer's day not a bird could be seen, till suddenly there was a quick 'jack-jack' above as a daw started from his hole or from where the great boughs joined the trunk. The squire's path went down the hollow till it deepened into a thinly wooded coomb, through which ran the streamlet coming from the wheatfields under the road. As the coomb opened, the squire went along a hedge near but not quite to the top. Years ago the coomb had been quarried for chalk, and the pits were only partly concealed by the bushes: the yellow spikes of wild mignonette flourished on the very edge, and even half way down the precipices. From the ledge above, the eye could see into these and into the recesses between the brushwood. The squire's son, Mr. Martin, used to come here with his rook-rifle, for he could always get a shot at a rabbit in the hollow. They could not see him approach; and the ball, if it missed, did no damage, being caught as in a bowl. Rifles in England, even when their range is but a hundred yards or so, are not be used without caution. Some one may be in the hedge nutting, or a labourer may be eating his luncheon in the shelter; it is never possible to tell who may be behind the screen of brambles through which the bullet slips so easily. Into these hollows Martin could shoot with safety. As for the squire, he did not approve of rifles. He adhered to his double-barrel; and if a buck had to be killed, he depended on his smooth-bore to carry a heavy ball forty yards with fair accuracy. The fawns were knocked over with a wire cartridge unless Mr. Martin was in the way — he liked to try a rifle. Even in summer the old squire generally had his double-barrel with him — perhaps he might come across a weasel, or a stoat, or a crow. That was his excuse; but, in fact, without a gun the woods lost half their meaning to him. With it he could

stand and watch the buck grazing in the glade, or a troop of fawns —
sweet little creatures — so demurely feeding down the grassy slope from
the beeches. Already at midsummer the nuts were full formed on the
beeches; the green figs, too, he remembered were on the old fig-tree
trained against the warm garden wall. The horse chestnuts showed the
little green knobs which would soon enlarge and hang all prickly, like the
spiked balls of a holy-water sprinkler, such as was once used in the wars.
Of old the folk, having no books, watched every living thing, from the
moss to the oak, from the mouse to the deer; and all that we know now
of animals and plants is really founded upon their acute and patient
observation. How many years it took even to find out a good salad may
be seen from ancient writings, wherein half the plants about the hedges
are recommended as salad herbs: dire indeed would be our consternation
if we had to eat them. As the beech-nuts appear, and the horse chestnuts
enlarge, and the fig swells, the apples turn red and become visible in the

leafy branches of the apple-trees. Like horses, deer are fond of apples, and in former times, when deer-stealing was possible, they were often decoyed with them.

There is no tree so much of the forest as the beech. On the verge of the woods the oaks are far apart, the ashes thin; the verge is like a wilderness and scrubby, so that the forest does not seem to begin till you have penetrated some distance. Under the beeches the forest begins at once. They stand at the edge of the slope, huge round boles rising from the mossy ground, wide fans of branches — a shadow under them, a greeny darkness beyond. There is depth there — depth to be explored, depth to hide in. If there is a path, it is arched over like a tunnel with boughs; you know not whither it goes. The fawns are sweetest in the sunlight, moving down from the shadow; the doe best partly in shadow, partly in sun, when the branch of a tree casts its interlaced work, fine as Algerian silverwork, upon the back; the buck best when he stands among the fern, alert, yet not quite alarmed — for he knows the length of his leap — his horns up, his neck high, his dark eye bent on you, and every sinew strung to spring away. One spot of sunlight, bright and white falls, falls through the branches upon his neck, a fatal place, or near it: a guide, that bright white spot, to the deadly bullet, as in old days to the crossbow bolt. It was needful even then to be careful of the aim, for the herd, as Shakespeare tells us, at once recognised the sound of a crossbow: the jar of the string tight-strained to the notch by the goat's-foot lever, the slight whiz of the missile, were enough to startle them and to cause the rest to swerve and pass out of range. Yet the crossbow was quiet indeed compared with the gun which took its place. The crossbow was the beginning of shooting proper, as we now understand it; that is, of taking an aim by the bringing of one point into a line with another. With the longbow aim indeed was taken, but quite differently, for if the arrow were kept waiting with the string drawn, the eye and the hand would not go true together. The quicker the arrow left the bow the moment that it was full drawn, the better the result. On the other hand, the arblast was in no haste, but was adjusted deliberately — so deliberately that it gave rise to a proverb: 'A fool's bolt is soon shot.' This could not apply to the longbow, with which the arrow was discharged swiftly, while an arblast was slowly brought to the level like a rifle. As it was hard to draw again, that added strength to the saying; but it arose from the deliberation with which a good crossbowman aimed. To the longbow the crossbow was the express rifle. The express delivers its bullet accurately point-blank — the bullet flies straight to its mark up to a certain distance. So the crossbow bolt flew point-blank, and thus its application to hunting when the deer were really killed for their venison. The hunter stole through the fern, or crept about the thickets — thickets and fern exactly like those here today — or waited Indian-like in ambush behind an oak as the herd fed that way, and, choosing the finest buck, aimed his bolt so as either to slay at once or to break the foreleg. Like the hare, if the foreleg is injured, deer cannot progress; if only the hindquarter is hit, there is no telling how far they may go. Therefore the crossbow, as enabling the hunter to choose the exact spot where his bolt should strike, became the weapon of the chase, and by its very perfection began the extermination of the deer. Instead of the hounds and the noisy hunt, any man who could use the crossbow could kill a buck. The longbow, of all weapons, requires the most practice, and practice begun in early youth. Some of the extraordinary feats attributed to the outlaws in the woods and to the archers of the ancient English army are quite possible, but must have necessitated the constant use of a bow from childhood, so that it became second nature. But almost any man who had strength to set a crossbow, with moderate practice, and any idea at all of shooting, could become a fairly good shot with it. From the crossbow to a gun was a comparatively easy step, and it was the knowledge of the power of the one that led to the quick introduction of the other. For gunpowder was hardly discovered before handguns were thought of, and no discovery ever spread so swiftly. Then the arquebus swept away the old English chase.

These deer exist by permission. They are protected with jealous care; or rather they have been protected so long that by custom they have grown semi-consecrated, and it is rare for anyone to think of touching them. The fawns wander, and a man, if he choose, might often knock one over with his axe as he comes home from his work. The deer browse up to the

very skirts of the farmhouse below, sometimes even enter the rick-yard, and once now and then, if a gate be left open, walk in and eat the pease in the garden. The bucks are still a little wilder, a little more nervous for their liberty, but there is no difficulty in stalking them to within forty or fifty yards. They have either lost their original delicacy of scent, or else do not respond to it, as the approach of a man does not alarm them, else it would be necessary to study the wind; but you may get thus near them without any thought of the breeze — no nearer; then, bounding twice or thrice, lifting himself each time as high as the fern, the buck turns half towards you to see whether his retreat should or should not be continued.

The fawns have come out from the beeches, because there is more grass on the slope and in the hollows, where trees are few. Under the trees in the forest proper there is little food for them. Deer, indeed, seem fonder of half-open places than of the wood itself. Thickets, with fern at the foot and spaces of sward between, are their favourite haunts. Heavily timbered land and impenetrable underwood are not so much resorted to. The deer here like to get away from the retreats which shelter them, to wander in the half-open grounds on that part of the park free to them, or, if possible, if they see a chance, out into the fields. Once now and then a buck escapes, and is found eight or ten miles away. If the pale were removed how quickly the deer would leave the close forest which in imagination is so associated with them! It is not their ideal. They would rather wander over the hills and along the river valleys. The forest is, indeed, and always would be their cover, and its shadows their defence; but for enjoyment they would of choice seek the sweet herbage, which does not flourish where the roots of trees and underwood absorb all the richness of the soil. The farther the trees are apart the better the forest pleases them. Those great instinctive migrations of wild animals which take place annually in America are not possible in England. The deer here cannot escape — solitary individuals getting free of course, now and then; they cannot move in a body, and it is not easy to know whether any such desire remains among them. So far as I am aware, there is no mention of such migrations in the most ancient times; but the omission proves nothing, for before the Normans, before the game laws and parks together came into existence, no-one who could write thought enough of the deer to notice their motions. The monks were engaged in chronicling the inroads of the pagans, or writing chronologies of the Roman Empire. On analogical grounds it would seem quite possible that in their original state the English deer did move from part to part of the country with the seasons. Almost all the birds, the only really free things in this country now, move, even those that do not quit the island; and why not the deer in the old time when all the woods were open to them? England is not a large country, but there are considerable differences in the climate and the time at which vegetation appears, quite sufficient of themselves to induce animals to move from place to place. We have no narrowing buffalo zone to lament, for our buffalo zone disappeared long ago. These parks and woods are islets of the olden time, dotted here and there in the midst of the most modern agricultural scenery. These deer and their ancestors have been confined within the pale for hundreds of years, and though in a sense free, they are in no sense wild. But the old power remains still. See the buck as he starts away, and jumps at every leap as high as the fern. He would give the hounds a long chase yet.

The fern is fully four feet tall, hiding a boy entirely, and only showing a man's head. The deer do not go through it unless startled; they prefer to follow a track already made, one of their own trails. It is their natural cover, and when the buckhounds meet near London the buck often takes refuge in one or other of the fern-grown commons of which there are many on the southern side. But fern is inimical to grass, and, while it gives them cover, occupies the place of much more pleasant herbage. As their range is limited, though they have here a forest of some extent as well as the park to roam over, they cannot always obtain enough in winter. In frost, when the grass will not grow, or when snow is on the ground, that which they can find is supplemented with hay. They are, in fact, foddered exactly the same as cattle. In some of the smaller parks they are driven into inclosures and fed altogether. This is not the case here. Perhaps it was through the foggers, as the labourers are called who fodder cattle and carry out the hay in the morning and evening, that deer poachers of old discovered that they could approach the deer by carrying a bundle of sweet-smelling hay, which overcame the scent of the body and baffled the buck's keen nostrils till the thief was within shot. The foggers, being about so very early in the morning — they are out at the dawn — have found out a good many game secrets in their time. If the deer were outside the forest at any hour it was sure to be when the dew was on the grass, and thus they noticed that with the hay truss on their heads they could walk up quite close occasionally. Foggers know all the game on the places where they work; there is not a hare or a rabbit, a pheasant or a partridge whose ways are not plain to them. There are no stories now of stags a century old (three would go back to Queen Elizabeth); they have gone, like other traditions of the forest, before steam and breechloader. Deer lore is all but extinct, the terms of venery known but to a few; few, indeed, could correctly name the parts of a buck if one were sent them. The deer are a picture only — a picture that lives and moves and is beautiful to look at, but must not be rudely handled. Still, they linger while the marten has disappeared, the polecat is practically gone, and the badger becoming rare. It is curious that the badger has lived on through sufferance for three centuries. Nearly three centuries ago, a chronicler observed that the badger would have been rooted out before his time had it not been for the parks. There was no great store of badgers then; there is no great store now. Sketches remain in old country-houses of the chase of the marten; you see the hounds all yelping round the foot of a tree, the marten up in it, and in the middle of the hounds the huntsman in top-boots and breeches. You can but smile at it. To Americans it must forcibly recall the treeing of a 'coon. The deer need keep no watch, there are no wolves to pull them down; and it is quite probable that the absence of any danger of that kind is the reason of their tameness even more than the fact that they are not chased by man. Nothing comes creeping stealthily through the fern, or hunts them through the night. They can slumber in peace. There is no larger beast of prey than a stoat, or a stray cat. But they retain their dislike of dogs, a dislike shared by cattle, as if they too dimly remembered a time when they had been hunted. The list of animals still living within the pale and

still wild is short indeed. Besides the deer, which are not wild, there are hares, rabbits, squirrels, two kinds of rat — the land and the water rat — stoat, weasel, mole and mouse. There are more varieties of mouse than of any other animal: these, the weakest of all, have escaped best, though exposed to so many enemies. A few foxes, and still fewer badgers, complete the list, for there are no other animals here. Modern times are fatal to all creatures of prey, whether furred or feathered; and so even the owls are less numerous, both in actual numbers and in variety of species, than they were even fifty years ago.

But the forest is not vacant. It is indeed full of happy life. Every hollow tree — and there are many hollow trees where none are felled — has its nest of starlings, or titmice, or woodpeckers. Woodpeckers are numerous, and amusing to watch. Woodpigeons and turtle-doves abound, the former in hundreds nesting here. Rooks, of course, and jackdaws — daws love hollow trees — jays, and some magpies. The magpie is one of the birds which have partly disappeared from the fields of England. There are

broad lands where not one is to be seen. Once looking from the road at two in a field, a gentleman who was riding by stopped his horse and asked, quite interested, 'Are those magpies?' I replied that they were. 'I have not seen any since I was a boy till now,' he said. Magpies are still plentiful in some places, as in old parks in Somerset, but they have greatly diminished in the majority of instances. There are some here, and many jays. These are handsome birds, and with the green woodpeckers give colour to the trees. Nightjars or fern-owls fly round the outskirts and through the open glades in the summer twilight. These are some of the forest birds. The rest visit the forest or live in it, but are equally common to hedgerow and copse. Woodpeckers, jays, magpies, owls and nightjars are all distinctly forest and park birds, and are continually with the deer. The lesser birds are the happier that there are fewer hawks and crows. The deer are not torn with the cruel tooth of hound or wolf, nor does the sharp arrow sting them. It is a little piece of olden England without its terror and bloodshed.

The fawns fed away down the slope and presently into one of the broad green open paths or drives, where the underwood on each side is lined with bramble and with trailing white rose, which loves to cling to bushes scarcely higher than itself. Their runners stretch out at the edges of the drive, so that from the underwood the mound of green falls aslant to the sward. This gradual descent from the trees and ash to the bushes of hawthorn, from the hawthorn to the bramble, thence to the rose and the grass, gives to the vista of the broad path a soft, graceful aspect.

After the fawns had disappeared, the squire went on and entered under the beeches from which they had emerged. He had not gone far before he struck and followed a path which wound between the beech trunks and was entirely arched over by their branches. Squirrels raced away at the sound of his footsteps, darting over the ground and up the stems of the trees in an instant. A slight rustling now and then showed that a rabbit had been startled. Pheasants ran too, but noiselessly, and pigeons rose from the boughs above. The woodpigeons rose indeed, but they were not much frightened, and quickly settled again. So little shot at, they felt safe, and only moved from habit.

He crossed several paths leading in various directions, but went on, gradually descending till the gable end of a farmhouse became visible through the foliage. The old red tiles were but a few yards distant from the boughs of the last beech, and there was nothing between the house and the forest but a shallow trench almost filled with dead brown leaves and edged with fern. Out from that trench, sometimes stealthily slipping between the flattened fern-stalks, came a weasel, and, running through the plantains and fringe-like mayweed or stray pimpernel which covered the neglected ground, made for the strawrick. Searching about for mice, he was certain to come across a hen's egg in some corner, perhaps in a hay-crib, which the cattle, now being in the meadow, did not use. Or a stronger stoat crept out and attacked anything that he fancied. Very often there was a rabbit sitting in the long grass which grows round under an old hayrick. He would sit still and let anyone pass who did not know of his presence, but those who were aware used to give the grass a kick if they went that way, when he would carry his white tail swiftly round the corner of the rick. In winter hares came nibbling at everything in the garden, and occasionally in summer, if they fancied a herb: they would have spoiled it altogether if free to stay there without fear of someone suddenly appearing.

Dogs there were in plenty, but all chained, except a few mere puppies which practically lived indoors. It was not safe to have them loose so near the wood, the temptation to wander being so very strong. So that, though there was a continual barking and long, mournful whines for liberty, the wild creatures came in time to understand that there was little danger, and the rabbit actually sat under the hayrick.

Pheasants mingled with the fowls, and, like the fowls, only ran aside out of the way of people. In early summer there were tiny partridge chicks about, which rushed under the coop. The pheasants sometimes came down to the kitchen door, so greedy were they. With the dogs and ponies, the pheasants and rabbits, the weasels and the stoats, and the ferrets in their hutches, the place seemed really to belong more to the animals than to the tenant.

The forest strayed indoors. Bucks' horns, feathers picked up, strange birds shot and stuffed, fossils from the sandpits, coins and pottery from the line of the ancient Roman road, all the odds and ends of the forest, were scattered about within. To the yard came the cows which, with bells about their necks, wandered into the fern, and the swine, which searched and rooted about for acorns and beech-mast in autumn. The men who dug in the sandpits or for gravel came this way in and out to their labour, and so did those who split up the fallen trunks into logs. Now and then a woodpecker came with a rush up from the meadows, where he had been visiting the hedgerows, and went into the forest with a yell as he entered the trees. The deer fed up to the precincts, and at intervals a buck at the dawn got into the garden. But the flies from the forest teased and terrified the horses, which would have run away with the heavily loaded waggon behind them if not protected with fine netting as if in armour. They did run away sometimes at harrow, tearing across the field like mad things. You could not keep the birds out of the garden, try how you would. They had most of the sowings up. The blackbirds pecked every apple in the orchard. How the dead leaves in autumn came whirling in thousands through rick-yard and court in showers upon the tiles! Nor was it of much avail to sweep them away; they were there again tomorrow, and until the wind changed. The swallows were now very busy building; there were not many houses for them, and therefore they flocked here. Up from over the meadows came the breeze, drawing into the hollow recesses of the forest behind. It came over the grass and farther away over corn just yellowing, the shadows of the clouds racing with it and instantly lost in the trees. It drew through the pillars of the forest, and away to the hills beyond.

The squire's ale was duly put for him, the particular gossip he liked was ready for him; and having taken both, he looked at his old watch and went on. His path now led for a while just inside the pale, which here divided the forest from the meadows. In the olden time it would have been made of oak, for they built all things then with an eye to endurance; but it was now of fir, pitched, sawn from firs thrown in the copses. For the purpose of keeping the deer in, it was as useful as the pale of oak. Oak is not so plentiful nowadays. The high spars were the special vaunting-places of the little brown wrens which perched there and sang, in defiance of all that the forest might hold. Rabbits crept under, but the hares waited till evening and went round by the gates. Presently the path turned and the squire passed a pond partly dried up, from the margin of which several pigeons rose up, clattering their wings. They are fond of the neighbourhood of water, and are sure to be there some time during the day. The path went upwards, but the ascent was scarcely perceptible through hazel bushes, which became farther apart and thinner as the elevation increased, and the soil was less rich. Some hawthorn bushes succeeded, and from among these he stepped out into the open park. Nothing could be seen of the manor-house here. It was hidden by the roll of the ground and the groups of trees. The close sward was already a little brown — the trampling of hoofs as well as the heat causes the brownish hue of fed sward, as if it were bruised. He went out into the park, bearing somewhat to the right and passing many hawthorns, round the trunks of which the grass was cut away in a ring by the hoofs of animals seeking shadow. Far away on a rising knoll a herd of deer were lying under some elms. In front were the downs, a mile or so distant; to the right, meadows and cornfields, towards which he went. There was no house nor any habitation in view; in the early part of the year, the lambing-time, there was a shepherd's hut on wheels in the fields, but it had been drawn away.

According to tradition, there is no forest in England in which a king has not hunted. A king, they say, hunted here in the old days of the crossbow; but happily the place escaped notice in that artificial era when half the parks and woods were spoiled to make the engraver's ideal landscape of straight vistas, broad in the foreground and narrowing up to nothing. Wide, straight roads — you can call them nothing else — were cut through the finest woods, so that upon looking from a certain window, or standing at a certain spot in the grounds, you might see a church tower at the end of the cutting. In some parks there are half-a-dozen such horrors shown to you as a great curiosity; some have a monument or pillar at the end. These hideous disfigurements of beautiful scenery should surely be wiped out in our day. The stiff, straight cutting could soon be filled up by planting, and after a time the woods would resume their natural condition. Many common highway roads are really delightful, winding through trees and hedgerows, with

glimpses of hills and distant villages. But these planned, straight vistas, radiating from a central spot as if done with ruler and pen, at once destroy the pleasant illusion of primeval forest. You may be dreaming under the oaks of the chase or of Rosalind: the moment you enter such a vista all becomes commonplace. Happily this park escaped, and it is beautiful. Our English landscape wants no gardening: it *cannot* be gardened. The least interference kills it. The beauty of English woodland and country is in its detail. There is nothing empty and unclothed. If the clods are left a little while undisturbed in the fields, weeds spring up and wild-flowers bloom upon them. Is the hedge cut and trimmed, lo the bluebells flower the more and a yet fresher green buds forth upon the twigs. Never was there a garden like the meadow: there is not an inch of the meadow in early summer without a flower. Old walls, as we saw just now, are not left without a fringe; on the top of the hardest brick wall, on the sapless tiles, on slates, stonecrop takes hold and becomes a cushion of yellow bloom. Nature is a miniature painter and handles a delicate brush, the tip of which touches the tiniest spot and leaves something living. The park has indeed its larger lines, its broad open sweep, and gradual slope, to which the eye accustomed to small inclosures requires time to adjust itself. These left to themselves are beautiful; they are the surface of the earth, which is always true to itself and needs no banks nor artificial hollows. The earth is right and the tree is right: trim either and all is wrong. The deer will not fit to them then.

The squire came near enough to the cornfield to see that the wheatears were beginning to turn yellow and that the barley had the silky appearance caused by the beard, the delicate lines of which divide the light and reflect it like gossamer. At some distance a man was approaching; he saw him, and sat down on the grass under an oak to await the coming of Ettles the keeper. Ettles had been his rounds and had visited the outlying copses, which are the special haunts of pheasants. Like the deer, pheasants, if they can, will get away from the main wood. He was now returning, and the squire, well knowing that he would pass this way, had purposely crossed his path to meet him. The dogs ran to the squire and at once made friends with him. Ettles, whose cheek was the colour of the oak-apples in spring, was more respectful: he stood till the squire motioned him to sit down. The dogs rolled on the sward, but, though in the shadow, they could not extend themselves sufficiently nor pant fast enough. Yonder the breeze that came up over the forest on its way to the downs blew through the group of trees on the knoll, cooling the deer as it passed.

Century Illustrated Monthly Magazine (New York & London), October 1888

Among the Nuts

THE NUTS are ripening once more, and it is almost the time to go a-gipsying — the summer passes like the shadow of a cloud which strikes the edge of the yellow wheat and comes over and is gone; it does not give you time to rub out a single ear of corn. Before it is possible to gather the harvest of thought and observation the summer has passed, and we must bind the hastily stitched book with the crimson leaves of autumn. Under these very hazel boughs only yesterday, i.e. in May, looking for cuckoo-sorrel, as the wood-sorrel is called, there rolled down a brown last year's nut from among the moss of the bank. In the side of this little brown nut, at its thicker end, a round hole had been made with a sharp tool which had left the marks of its chiselling. Through this hole the kernel had been extracted by the skilful mouse. Two more nuts were found on the same bank, bored by the same carpenter. The holes looked as if he had turned the nut round and round as he gnawed. Unless the nut had shrunk, the hole was not large enough to pull the kernel out all at once; it must have been eaten little by little in many mouthfuls. The same amount of nibbling would have sawn a circle round the nut, and so, dividing the shell in two, would have let the kernel out bodily — a plan more to our fancy; but the mouse is a nibbler, and he preferred to nibble, nibble, nibble. Hard by one afternoon, as the cows were lazily swishing their tails coming home to milking, and the shadow of the thick hedge had already caused the anemones in the grass to close their petals, there was a slight rustling sound. Out into the cool grass by some cowslips there came a small dark head. It was an adder, verily a snake in the grass and flowers. His quick eye — you know the proverb, 'If his ear were as quick as his eye, No man should pass him by' — caught sight of us immediately, and he turned back. The hedge was hollow there, and the mound grown over with close-laid, narrow-leaved ivy. The viper did not sink in these leaves, but slid with a rustling sound fully exposed above them. His grey length and the chain of black diamond spots down his back, his flat head with deadly tooth, did not harmonise as the green snake does with leaf and grass. He was too marked, too prominent — a venomous foreign thing, fit for tropic sands and nothing English or native to our wilds. He seemed like a reptile that had escaped from the glass case of some collection.

The green snake or grass snake, with yellow-marked head, fits in perfectly with the floating herbage of the watery places he frequents. The eye soon grows accustomed to his curves, till he is no more startling than a frog among the water-crowfoot you are about to gather. To the adder the mind never becomes habituated; he ever remains repellent. This adder was close to a house and cowshed, and, indeed, they seem to like to be near cows. Since then a large silvery slow-worm was killed just there — a great pity, for they are perfectly harmless. We saw, too, a very large

lizard under the heath. Three little effets (efts) ran into one hole in the bank yesterday. Some of the men in spring went off into the woods to 'flawing,' i.e. to barking the oak which is thrown in May — the bark is often used now for decoration, like the Spanish cork bark. Some were talking already of the 'grit' work and looking forward to it, that is, to mowing and haymaking, which mean better wages. The farmers were grumbling that their oats were cuckoo oats, not sown till the cuckoo cried, and not likely to come to much. So, indeed, it fell out, for the oats looked very thin and spindly when the nuts turned rosy again. At work hoeing among the 'kelk' or 'kilk,' the bright yellow charlock, the labourers stood up as the cuckoo flew over singing, and blew cuckoo back to him in their hollow fists. This is a trick they have, something like whistling in the fist, and so naturally done as to deceive anyone. The children had been round with the May garland, which takes the place of the Maypole, and is carried slung on a stick, and covered with a white cloth, between two little girls. The cloth is to keep the dust and sun from spoiling the flowers — the rich golden kingcups and the pale anemones trained about two hoops, one within the other. They take the cloth off to

show you the garland, and surely you must pay them a penny for thought of old England. Yet there are some who would like to spoil this innocent festival. I have heard of some wealthy people living in a village who do their utmost to break up the old custom by giving presents of money to all the poor children who will go to school on that day instead of a-Maying. A very pitiful thing truly! Give them the money, and let they go a-Maying as well. The same bribe they repeat at Christmas to stay the boys from going round mumming. It is in spring that the folk make most use of herbs, such as herb tea of gorse bloom. One cottage wife exclaimed that she had no patience with women so ignorant they did not know how to use herbs, as wood-sage or wood-betony. Most of the gardens have a few plants of the milky-veined holy thistle — good, they say, against inflammations, and in which they have much faith. Soon after the May garlands the meadow orchis comes up, which is called 'dead men's hands', and after that the 'ram's-horn' orchis, which has a twisted petal; and in the evening the bat, which they call flittermouse, appears again.

The light is never the same on a landscape many minutes together, as all know who have tried, ever so crudely, to fix the fleeting expression of the earth with pencil. It is ever changing, and in the same way as you walk by the hedges day by day there is always some fresh circumstance of nature, the interest of which in a measure blots out the past. This morning we found a bramble leaf, something about which has for the moment put the record of months aside. This bramble leaf was marked with a grey streak, which coiled and turned and ran along beside the midrib, forming a sort of thoughtless design, a design without an idea. The Greek fret seems to our eyes in its regularity and its repetition to have a human thought in it. The coils and turns upon this leaf like many other markings of nature, form a designless design, the idea of which is not traceable back to a mind. They are the work of a leaf-boring larva which has eaten its way between the two skins of the leaf, much like boring a tunnel between the two surfaces of a sheet of paper. If you take a needle you can insert the point in the burrow and pass it along wherever the bore is straight, so that the needle lies between the two sides of the leaf. Off hand, if anyone were asked if it were possible to split a leaf, he would say no. This little creature, however, has worked along inside it, and lived there. The upper surface of the leaf is a darker green, and seems to the touch a firmer texture than the lower; there are no marks on the under surface, which does not seem touched, so that what the creature has really done is to split one surface. He has eaten long underneath it, raising it no doubt a little by the thickness of his body, as if you crept between the carpet and the floor. The softer undersurface representing the floor is untouched. The woodbine leaves are often bored like this, and seem to have patterns traced upon them. There is no particle of matter so small but that it seems to have a living thing working at it and resolving it into still more minute atoms; nothing so insignificant but that upon examination it will be found to be of the utmost value to something alive. Upon almost every fir branch near the end there are little fragments like cotton, so thick in places as to quite hang the boughs with threads; these gossamer-like fragments appear to be left by some insect, perhaps an aphis; and it is curious to note how very busy the little

willow-wrens are in the fir boughs. They are constantly at work there; they sing in the firs in the earliest spring, they stay there all the summer, and now that the edge of autumn approaches their tiny beaks are still picking up insects the whole day long. The insects they devour must be as numerous as the fir needles that lie inches thick on the ground in the copse.

Across a broad, dry, sandy path, worn firm, some thousands of ants passing to and fro their nest had left a slight trail. They were hurrying on in full work, when I drew the top of my walking-stick across their road, obliterating about an inch of it. In an instant the work of the nest was stopped, and thousands upon thousands of factory hands were thrown out of employment. The walking-stick had left two little ridges of sand like minute parallel earthworks drawn across their highway. Those that came out of the nest on arriving at the little ridge on their side immediately stopped, worked their antennae in astonishment, then went up to the top of it, and seemed to try to look round. After a moment they ran back and touched those that were coming on to communicate the intelligence. Every ant that came did exactly the same thing; not one of them passed the little ridge, but all returned. By and by the head of the column began to spread out and search right and left for the lost track. They scouted this way and they scouted that, they turned and doubled and went through every possible evolution, hundreds of them, sometimes a score at once, yet not one of them attempted to go straight forward, which would have brought them into their old path. It was scarcely thrice the length of an ant's body to where their path began again; they could not see or scent, or in any way find out what was so short a distance in front of them. The most extraordinary thing was that not one ventured to explore straight forward; it was as if their world came to an end at that little ridge, and they were afraid to step into chaos. The same actions were going on behind the other ridge of sand just opposite, an inch away. There the column of ants that had been out foraging was met with a like difficulty, and could not find their way. There, too, hundreds of ants were exploring right and left in every direction except straight forward, in a perfect buzz of excitement. Once or twice an ant from either party happened to mount on the parallel ridges at the same time, and if they had strained forward and stretched out their antennae they could have almost touched each other. Yet they seemed quite unconscious of each other's presence. Unless in a well-worn groove a single ant appears incapable of running in a straight line. At first their motions searching about suggested the action of a pack of hounds making a cast; hounds, however, would have very soon gone forward and so picked up the trail.

If I may make a guess at the cause of this singular confusion, I think I should attribute it to some peculiarity in the brain of the ant, or else to some consideration of which we are ignorant, but which weighs with ants, and not to any absence of the physical senses. Because they do not do as we should do under similar circumstances is no proof that they do not possess the power to hear and see. Experiments, for instance, have been made with bees to find out if they have any sense of hearing, by shouting close to a bee, drawing discordant notes on the violin, striking pieces of metal together, and so on, to all of which the bee remained indifferent. What else could she do? Neither of these sounds hurt if she heard them, nor seemed to threaten danger; they simply conveyed no impression at all to her mind. Observe your favourite pussy curled up in the armchair at such time as she knows the dishes have been cleared away, and there is no more chance of wheedling a titbit from you. You may play the piano, or the violin, or knock with a hammer, or shout your loudest, she will take no notice, no more than if she actually had no ears at all. Are you, therefore, to conclude she does not hear you? As well conclude that people do not hear the thunder because they do not shout in answer to it. Such noises simply do not concern her, and she takes no notice. Now, though her eyes be closed, let a strange dog run in, and at the light pad pad of his feet, scarcely audible on the carpet, she is up in a moment, blazing with wrath. That is a sound that interests her. So, too, perhaps it may be with ants and bees, who may hear and see, and yet take no apparent notice because the circumstances are not interesting, and the experiment is to them unintelligible. Fishes in particular have been often, I think, erroneously judged in this way, and have been considered deaf, and to have little intelligence, while in truth the fact is we have not discovered a way of communicating with them any more than they have found a way of talking with us. Fishes, I know, are keener of sight than I am when they are interested, and I believe they can hear equally well, and are not by any means without mind. These ants that acted so foolishly to appearance may have been influenced by some former experience of which we know nothing; there may be something in the past history of the ant which may lead them to profoundly suspect interference with their path as indicative of extreme danger. Once, perhaps, many ant-generations ago, there was some creature which acted thus in order to destroy them. This, of course, is merely an illustration put forward to suggest the idea that there may be a reason in the brain of the ant of which we know nothing. I do not know that I myself am any more rational, for looking back along the path of life I can see now how I turned and twisted and went to the right and the left in the most crooked manner, putting myself to endless trouble, when by taking one single step straight forward in the right direction, if I had only known, I might have arrived at once at the goal. Can any of us look beyond the little ridge of one day and see what will happen the day after? Some hours afterwards, towards evening, I found the ants were beginning to get over their difficulty. On one side an ant would go forward in a half-circle, on the other another ant would advance sideways, and meeting together they would touch their antennae, and then the first would travel back with the second, and so the line was re-established. It was very much as if two batsmen at opposite wickets should run forward each halfway, and after shaking hands and conversing, one of them should lead the other safely over.

The Scots Observer, 23 August 1886

Field Sports in Art

T HE MOST ancient attempt to delineate the objects of sport in existence is, I think, the celebrated engraving of a mammoth on a portion of a mammoth's tusk. I call it an engraving because the figure is marked out with incised lines such as the engraver makes with his tool, and it is perfect enough to print from. If it were inked and properly manipulated it would leave an impression — an artist's proof, the most curious and extraordinary in the world, for the block was cut with flint instruments by cavemen an incredible number of years ago, perhaps before England was separated from the Continent by the sea, while the two were still connected, and it was dry land where now the *Calais-Douvres* steams so steadily over the waves. But it would be an artist's proof with the lights and shades reversed, the lines that sketch the form of the mammoth would be white and the body dark, yet for all that lifelike, since the undulating indentations that represent the wholly hide of the immense creature would relieve the ground. This picture of a prehistoric animal, drawn by a prehistoric artist, shows that Art arose from the chase. Traced to the den of primeval man, who had no Academy to instruct him, no Ruskin to guide, and no gallery to exhibit in, it appears that Art sprang from nature, and not from science. His life was occupied with the hunt, and he represented that which filled his thoughts. Those who understand wild sports will not for a moment doubt that the mammoth was taken in pits or otherwise destroyed despite its huge strength; no matter if it had been twice as large, the cunning of man would have been equal to the difficulty. The mind is the arrow that slays the monster. The greater the danger the greater the interest, and consequently the more the imagination would dwell upon the circumstances of the chase. Afterwards resting in the cave round about the fire and thinking of the mighty work of sport which had been accomplished, the finger of the savage would involuntarily describe the outline of the creature so laboriously captured. His finger might describe it upon the scattered ashes whitening the ground beside him. Or it might describe the outline simply in the air. Speech in its inception was so much expressed by the finger as the tongue; perhaps the fingers talked before the mouth, and in a sense writing preceded language. Uttering the unpolished sound which in their primitive society indicated the mammoth, the savage drew rapidly a figure with his finger, and his companions read his meaning written in the air. To this day it is common for the Italian peasantry to talk with their fingers; a few syllables suffice, illustrated and emphasised by those dexterous hands. A more subtle meaning is thus conveyed than could be put in words. Some of the most ancient languages seem bald and incomplete, too rigid; they need intonation, as it were, to express passion or changes of emotion, and when written the letters are too far apart to indicate what is meant. Not too far apart upon the page, but far apart in their sense, which has to be supplied as you supply the vowels. In actual use such languages must have required much gesture and finger-sketching in the air. The letters of the Egyptians largely consist of animals and birds, which represent both sounds and ideas. Dreaming over the embers of his fire, the caveman saw pass before his mental vision all the circumstances of the chase, ending with the crash when the mammoth crashed into the pit, at which he would start and partially awake. Intentness of mind upon a pursuit causes an equivalent intentness of dream, and thus wild races believe their dreams to be real and substantial things, and not mere shadows of the night. To those who do not read or write much, even in our days, dreams are much more real than to those who are continuously exercising the imagination. If you use your imagination all day you will not fear it at night. Since I have been occupied with literature my dreams have lost

all vividness and are less real than the shadows of trees, they do not deceive me even in my sleep. At every hour of the day I am accustomed to call up figures at will before my eyes, which stand out well-defined and coloured to the very hue of their faces. If I see these or have disturbed visions during the night they do not affect me in the least. The less literary a people, the more they believe in dreams; the disappearance of superstition is not due to the cultivation of reason or the spread of knowledge, but purely to the mechanical effect of reading, which so perpetually puts figures and aerial shapes before the mental gaze that in time those that occur naturally are thought no more of than those conjured into existence by a book. It is in far-away country places, where people read very little, that they see phantoms and consult the oracles of fate. Their dreams are real.

The mammoth came through his cave before the embers of his fire — the sleeping savage could touch it with his flint-headed spear — there was the crash as it fell into the prepared pit; he awakes, the dying embers cast shadows on the walls, and in these he traces the shape of the vast creature hastening away. The passing spirit has puffed the charred brands into a second's flame, and thus shadowed itself in the hollow of the cavern.

Deeper than the excitement of the chase lies that inner consciousness which dwells upon and questions itself — the soul of the caveman pondered upon itself; the question came to him, as he crouched in the semi-darkness, over the fire which he had stirred, 'Will my form and aerial shadow live on after my death like that which passed but now? Shall I, too, be a living dream?' The reply was, 'Yes, I shall continue to be; I shall start forth from my burial-mound upon the chase in the shadow-land just as now I start forth from my cave. I shall entrap the giant woolly elephant — I shall rejoice at his capture; we shall triumph yet again and again. Let then my spear and knife be buried with me, but chip them first — kill them — that I may use their spirit likenesses in the dream-chase.'

With a keen-edged splinter of flint in the daylight he incised the outlines of the mammoth upon a smooth portion of its tusk — its image was associated with his thoughts of a future life, and thus Art in its earliest inception represented the highest aspirations of man.

But could the ignorant savage of that long-lost day have been capable of such work? The lowest race of savages in Southern Africa — the Bushmen — go about with festoons of entrails wound around their loins. After a successful hunt — with the pit or poisoned arrows — they remove the entrails of the slain animal and wear them like coronals for present ornament and future regalement. These creatures are nevertheless artists. On the walls of caves they have painted the antelope and the lion in bright colours; they have not only caught the shape and hue of the animals about them, but their action and movement. The figures are in motion, skilfully drawn and full of spirit.

If anyone asks, 'Is the application of Art to the chase really so old, so very very old, as this?' I refer them to the stars. How long ago is it since the constellations received their names? At what date were they first arranged in groups? Upon the most ancient monuments and in the most ancient writings they have the same forms assigned to them as at this day, and that too in countries remote from each other. The signs of the Zodiac are almost as old as the stars themselves; that is, as old as the time when the stars were first beheld of human eyes. Amongst them there is the Archer — Sagittarius — the chase in the shape of man; greatest and grandest of all the constellations is Orion, the mightly hunter, and giant who slew the wild beasts by strength. There is no assemblage of stars so brilliant as those which compose the outline of Orion; the Hunter takes the first place in the heavens. Art exists in the imagination — imagination drew lines from star to star, and repeated its life on earth in the sky.

So it is true that the first picture — whether drawn by the imagination alone in the constellations, on the walls of the cave with ochre and similar materials, or engraved with keen splinters of flint on the mammoth's tusk — the first picture was of the chase. Animals are earliest, the human form next, flowers and designs and stories in drawings next, and landscape last of all. Landscape is peculiarly the art of the moderns — it is the art of *our* civilisation; no other civilisation seems to have cared for it. Towers and castles are indeed seen on the bas-reliefs of Assyria, and waving lines indicate rivers, but these are merely subsidiary, and to give place and locality to the victories the king is achieving. The battle is the interest, the landscape merely the stage. Till the latter days of European life the artist took no notice of landscape.

The painting of hills and rocks and rivers, woods and fields, is of recent date, and even in these scenes the artist finds it necessary to place some animals or birds. Even now he cannot ignore the strong love of human beings for these creatures; if they are omitted the picture loses its interest to the majority of eyes. Everyone knows how wonderfully popular the works of Landseer have been, and he was an animal painter, and his subjects chiefly suggested by sport. The same spirit that inspired the cave-dweller to engrave the mammoth on the slab of ivory still lives in the hearts of men.

There is a beautiful etching of 'The Poacher' (to which I shall have to recur); he is in the wood, and his dog is watching his upraised finger. From that finger the dog learns everything. He knows by its motion when to start, which way to go, what to do, whether to be quick or slow, to return or to remain away. He understands his master quite as well as if they conversed in human speech. He enters into the spirit of the enterprise. 'If you want your business done, go; if not, send,' is true only of men. The poacher wants his business done, and he sends his agent — his dog — certain that it will be done for him better than he could do it himself. The dog is conscientious, he will omit nothing, he will act as if his master's eye was on him the whole time. Now this attitude of the dog's mind is so exquisitely rendered in the picture that he seems verily to speak with intelligence. I love that dog though he does but exist in ink; he is the true image of a real dog, and his mind shines through his body. This effect upon me as the spectator is produced by a clever arrangement of lines upon the plate from which the etching was printed, thin lines cut into the copper with curious sharp tools, behind a screen of tissue-paper to shield the eyes from the light, done in the calm of the studio, thoughtfully, with artistic skill. Given the original genius to conceive such a dog, the knowledge, how to express the ideas, and the tools to work with, and we see how it became possible to execute the etching. But suppose the artist was supplied with a piece of smooth ivory for his plate, and a sharp penknife for his etching needle, and set behind a boulder to watch the mammoth and sketch it by incision on the ivory, and there would be produced very much the same kind of picture as the caveman made. It could not have the delicate shading, the fine edge, the completion and finish of the dog; it could not visibly think as that dog thinks. It would consist of a few quick strong dashes, conveying the weight and force and image of the elephant in as few strokes as possible. It would be a charcoal sketch; broad and powerful lines that do not themselves delineate, but compel your imagination to do the picture in your mind, so that you see a great deal more than is drawn. So the caveman was really a great artist — his intense interest in the chase supplied the lack of academics and scientific knowledge and galleries to copy from. This primeval picture thus tells you that the highly educated artist of the present day, removed from his accessories, away from his liquid colours, easels, canvas, prepared paper, and so forth, can only do

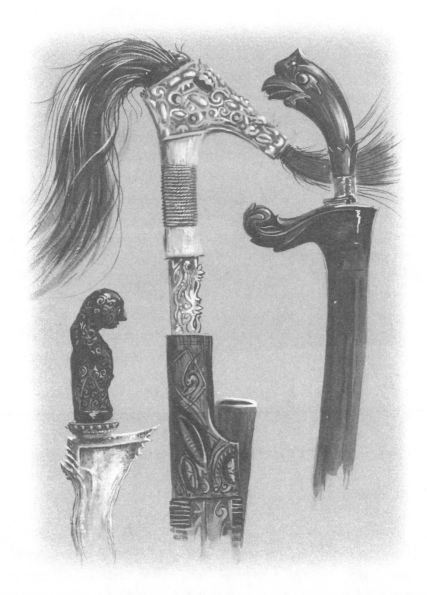

'Wild races carve or ornament their weapons'

what the caveman did. But still further, he can only do that if he possesses great natural genius — only a man who could draw the poacher's dog could do it. Those who depend altogether on the prepared paper and liquid colours, patent easel and sketching stool, could simply do nothing.

It is nearly certain that if the primeval man sketched the mammoth he likewise carved his spear-shaft, the haft of his knife, the handle of his 'celt', that chisel-like weapon whose shape so closely resembles the front teeth. The 'celt' is a front tooth in flint or bronze, enlarged and fitted to a handle for chipping, splitting, and general work. In museums celts are sometimes fitted to a handle to show how they were used, but the modern adapter has always overlooked the carving. Wild races whose time is spent in sport or war — very nearly synonymous terms — always carve or ornament their weapons, their canoes, the lintels of their doors, the posts of their huts. There is in this the most singular difference from the ways of landscape civilisation. Things that we use are seldom ornamented — our tables, our chairs, our houses, our carriages, our everything is as plain as plain can be. Or if ornamented, it is ornamented in a manner that seems to bear no kind of relation to the article or its uses, and to rouse no sympathies whatever. For instance, our plates — some have the willow pattern, some designs of blackberry bushes, and I really cannot see what possible connection the bushes or the Chinese summerhouses have with the roast beef of old England or the côtelette of France. The last relic of Art carving is visible round about a bread platter, here and there wreaths of wheatears; very suitable these to a platter bearing bread formed of corn. Alas! I touched one of these platters one day to feel the grain of the wood, and it was cold earthenware — cold, ungenial, repellent crockery, a mockery, sham! Now the original wooden platter was, I think, true Art, and the crockery copy is not Art. The primeval savage, without doubt, laboriously cut out a design, or at least gave some curve and shape to the handle of his celt or the shaft of his spear, and the savages at this day as laboriously carve their canoes. The English sportsman, however, does not cut, or carve, or in any way shape his gun-stock to his imagination. The stock is as smooth and as plain as

polished wood can be. There is a sort of speckling on the barrels, and there is a conventional design on the lock-plate; conventional, indeed, in the most blasé sense of the word — quite blasé and worn out, this scratch of intertwisted lines, not so much as a pheasant even engraved on the lock-plate; it is a mere killing machine, this gun, and there is no Art, thought or love of nature about it. Sometimes the hammers are filed, little notches crossing, and there imagination stops. The workman can get no farther than his file will go, and you know how that acts to and fro in a straight groove. A pheasant or hare at full speed, a few trees — firs as most characteristic — could be put on the plate, and something else on the trigger guard; firs are easily drawn, and make most appearance for a few touches; pheasants roost in them. Even a coat of arms, if it were the genuine coat of arms of the owner's family, would look well. Men have their book-plates and stamp their library volumes, why not a gun design? As many sportsmen scarcely see their guns for three-fourths of the year, it is possible to understand that the gun becomes a killing machine merely to them, to be snatched up and thrown aside the instant its office is over. But the gamekeeper carries his gun the year through, and sits in the room with it when indoors, still he never even so much as scratches an outline of his favourite dog on it. In these landscape days we put our pictures on the walls only, and no imagination into the things we handle and use. A good deal of etching might be done on a gun, most of it being metal, while more metal could be easily inlaid for the purpose. Etching, I suppose, is the right word; at all events, designs, records of actual sporting feats, or outlines of favourite sporting places — nooks in the woods, falls of the stream, deep combes of the hills — could be cut in with aqua fortis. So many draw or paint nowadays, and in this manner they could make some use of their skill, drawing perhaps for those who only understand the use of cartridge paper when it has gunpowder inside it. Sportsmen see the very best of scenery, and come across old hollow trunks and curious trees, effects, and 'bits' of every kind, from a twisted hawthorn to an antlered stag; if they could get an artistic friend to see these, there would be some good gun-etchings done.

Art Journal, April 1885

The Countryside: Sussex

O N THE wall of an old barn by the great doors there still remains a narrow strip of noticeboard, much battered and weather-beaten: 'Beware of steel —.' can be read, the rest has been broken off, but no doubt it was 'traps'. 'Beware of steel traps', a caution to thieves — a reminiscence of those old days which many of our present writers and leaders of opinion seem to think never existed. When the strong labourer could hardly earn 7/- a week, when in some parishes scarcely half the population got work at all, living, in the most literal sense, on the parish, when bread was dear and the loaf was really life itself, then that stern inscription had meaning enough. The wheat was threshed by the flail in full view of the wretched, who could gaze through the broad doors at the golden grain; the sparrows helped themselves, men

160

dare not. At night men tried to steal the corn and had to be prevented by steel traps, like rats. Today wheat is so cheap, it scarcely pays to carry it to market. Some farmers have it ground, and sell the flour direct to the consumer; some have used it for feeding purposes — actually for hogs. The contrast is extraordinary. Better let the hogs eat the corn than that man should starve. Today the sparrows are just as busy as ever of old, chatter, chirp around the old barn, while the threshing machine hums, and every now and then lowers its voice in a long-drawn descending groan of seemingly deep agony. Up it rises again as the sheaves are cast in — hum, hum, hum; the note rises and resounds and fills the yard up to the roof of the barn and the highest tops of the ricks as a flood fills a pool, and overflowing, rushes abroad over the fields, past the red hop-oast, past the copse of yellowing larches, onwards to the hills. An inarticulate music — a chant telling of the sunlit hours that have gone and the shadows that floated under the clouds over the beautiful wheat. No more shall the tall stems wave in the wind or listen to the bees seeking the clover-fields. The lark that sang above the green corn, the partridge that sheltered among the yellow stalks, the list of living things delighting in it — all have departed. The joyous life of the wheat is

Cottager calls her cat and shakes them out of her skirts

ended — not in vain, for now the grain becomes the life of man, and in that object yet more glorified. Outwards the chant extending, reaches the hollows of the valley, rolling over the shortened stubble, where the plough already begins the first verse of a new time. A pleasant sound to listen to, the hum of the threshing, the beating of the engine, the rustle of the straw, the shuffle shuffle of the machine, the voices of the men, the occupation and bustle in the autumn afternoon! I listened to it sitting in the hop-oast, whose tower, like a castle turret, overlooks and domineers the yard. In the loft the resounding hum whirled around, beating and rebounding from the walls, and forcing its way out again through the narrow window. The edge, as it were, of a sunbeam lit up the rude chamber crossed with unhewn beams and roofed above with unconcealed tiles, whose fastening pegs were visible. A great heap of golden scales lay in one corner, the hops fresh from the drying. Up to his waist in a pocket let through the floor a huge giant of a man trod the hops down in the sack, turning round and round, and now his wide shoulders and now his red cheeks succeeded. The music twirled him about as a leaf by the wind. Without the rich blue autumn sky; within the fragrant odour of hops, the hum of the threshing circling round like the buzz of an immense bee. As the hum of insects high in the atmosphere of midsummer suits and fits to the roses and the full green meads, so the hum of the threshing suits to the yellowing leaf and drowsy air of autumn. The iteration of hum and monotone soothes, and means so much more in its inarticulation than the adjusted chords and tune of written music. Laughing, the children romped round the ricks; they love the threshing and flock to it, they watch the flywheel rotating, they look in at the furnace door when the engine-driver stokes his fire, they gaze wonderingly at the gauge, and long to turn the brass taps; then with a shout they rush to chase the unhappy mice dislodged from the corn. The mice hide themselves in the petticoats of the women working at the 'sheening', and the cottager when she goes home in the evening calls her cat and shakes them out of her skirts. By a blue waggon the farmer stands leaning on his staff. He is an invalid, and his staff, or rather pole, is as tall as himself; he holds it athwart, one end touching the ground beyond his left foot, the other near his right shoulder. His right hand grasps it rather high, and his left down by his hip, so that the pole forms a line across his body. In this way he is steadied and supported and his whole weight relieved, much more so than it would be with an ordinary walking-stick or with one in each hand. When he walks he keeps putting the staff, which he calls a bat, in front, and so poles himself along. There is an invalid boy in the yard, who walks with a similar stick. The farmer is talking with a friend who has looked in from the lane in passing, and carries a two-spean spud, or Canterbury hoe, with points instead of a broad blade. They are saying that it is a 'pretty day', 'pretty weather' — it is always 'pretty' with them, instead of fine. Pretty weather for the hopping; and so that leads on to climbing up into the loft and handling the golden scales. The man with the hoe dips his brown fist in the heap and gathers up a handful, noting as he does so how the crisp, brittle, leaf-like substance of the hops crackles, and yet does not exactly break in his palm. They must be dry, yet not too dry to go to powder. They cling a little to the fingers, adhering to the skin, sticky. He looks for rust and finds none, and pronounces it a good sample. 'But there beant nothen' now like they old Grapes used to be', he concludes. The pair have not long gone down the narrow stairs when a waggon stops outside in the lane, and up comes the carter to speak with the 'drier' — the giant trampling round in the pocket — and to see how the hops 'be getting on'. In five minutes another waggoner looks in, then a couple of ploughboys, next a higgler passing by; no-one walks or rides or drives past the hop-kiln without calling to see how things are going on. The carters cannot stay long, but the boys linger, eagerly waiting a chance to help the 'drier', even if only to reach him his handkerchief from the nail. Round and round in the pocket brings out the perspiration, and the dust of the hops gets into the air-passages and thickens on the skin of his face. One of the lads has to push the hops towards him with a rake. 'Don't you step on 'em too much, that'll break 'em.' On the light breeze that comes now and then a little chaff floats in at the open window from the threshing. A crooked sort of face appears in the doorway, the body has halted halfway up — a semi-gipsy face — and the fellow thrusts a basket before him on the floor. 'Want any herrings?' 'No, thankie — no,' cries the giant. 'Not today, measter; thusty enough without they.' Herrings are regularly carried round in hoptime to all the gardens, and there is a great sale for them among the pickers. By degrees the 'drier' rises higher in the pocket, coming up, as it were, through the floor — first his shoulders, then his body, and now his knees are visible. This is the ancient way of filling a hop pocket; a machine is used now in large kilns, but here, where there is only one cone, indicative of a small garden, the old method is followed.

The steps on which I sit lead up to the door of the cone. Inside, the green hops lie on the horsehair carpet, and the fumes of the sulphur burning underneath come up through them. A vapour hangs about the surface of the hops; looking upwards, the diminishing cone rises hollow to the cowl, where a piece of blue sky can be seen. Round the cone a strip of thin lathing is coiled on a spiral; could anyone stand on these steps and draw the inside of the cone? Could perspective be so managed as to give the idea of the diminishing hollow and spiral? The side opposite would not be so difficult, but the bit this side, overhead and almost perpendicular, and so greatly foreshortened, how with that? It would be necessary to make the spectator of the drawing feel as if this side of the cone rose up from behind his head; as if his head were just inside the cone. Would not this be as curious a bit of study as any that could be found in the interior of old Continental churches, which people go so many miles to see? Our own land is so full of interest. There are pictures by the oldest Master everywhere in our own country, by the very Master of the masters, by Time, whose crooked signature lies in the corner of the shadowy farmhouse hearth.

Beneath the loft, on the ground floor, I found the giant's couch. The bed of a cart had been taken off its wheels, forming a very good bedstead, dry and sheltered on three sides. On the fourth the sleeper's feet were towards the charcoal fire. Opening the furnace door, he could sit there and watch the blue and green tongues of sulphur flame curl round about and above the glowing charcoal, the fumes rising to the hops on the horsehair high over. The 'hoppers' in the garden used to bring their

kettles and pots to boil, till the practice grew too frequent, and was
stopped, because the constant opening of the furnace wasted the heat.
The sulphur comes in casks. A sulphur cask sawn down the middle, with
a bit left by the head for cover, is often used by the hoppers as a cradle.
Another favourite cradle is made from a trug basket, the handle cut off. It
is then like half a large eggshell, with cross pieces underneath to prevent
it from canting aside. This cradle is set on the bare ground in the garden;
when they move one women takes hold of one end and a second of the
other, and thus carry the infant. If you ask them, they will find you a
'hop-dog', a handsome green caterpillar marked with black velvet strips
and downy bands between. Their labour usually ends early in the
afternoon.

The giant at the kiln must watch and bide his time the night through
till the hops are ready to be withdrawn from the cone. He is alone. Deep
shadows gather round the farmstead and the ricks, and there is not a
sound, nothing but the rustle of a leaf falling from the hollow oak by the
gateway. But at midnight, just as the drier is drawing the hops, a
thunderstorm bursts, and the blue lightning lights up the red cone
without, blue as the sulphur flames creeping over the charcoal within. It
is lonely work for him in the storm. By day he has many little things to

do between the greater labours, to make the pockets (or sacks) by sewing the sackcloth, or to mark the name of the farmer and the date with stencil plates. For sewing up the mouth of the pocket when filled there is a peculiar kind of string used; you may see it hanging up in any of the country 'stores'; they are not shops, but stores of miscellaneous articles. He must be careful not to fill his pockets too full of hops, not to tread them too closely, else the sharp folk in the market will suspect that unfair means have been resorted to to increase the weight, and will cut the pocket all to pieces to see if it contains a few bricks. Nor must it be too light; that will not do.

In this district, far from the great historic hop-fields of Kent, the hops are really grown in gardens, little pieces often not more than half an acre or even less in extent. Capricious as a woman, hops will only flourish here and there; they have the strongest likes and dislikes, and experience alone finds out what will suit them. These gardens are always on a slope, if possible in the angle of a field and under shelter of a copse, for the wind is the terror, and a great gale breaks them to pieces; the bines are bruised, bunches torn off, and poles laid prostrate. The gardens being so small, from five to forty acres in a farm, of course but few pickers are required, and the hop-picking becomes a 'close' business, entirely confined to home families, to the cottagers working on the farm and their immediate friends. Instead of a scarcity of labour, it is a matter of privilege to get a bin allotted to you. There are no rough folk down from Bermondsey or Mile End way. All staid, stay-at-home, labouring people — no riots; a little romping no doubt on the sly, else the maids would not enjoy the season so much as they do. But there are none of those wild hordes which collect about the greater fields of Kent. Farmers' wives and daughters and many very respectable girls go out to hopping, not so much for the money as the pleasant out-of-door employment, which has an astonishing effect on the health. Pale cheeks begin to glow again in the hopfields. Children who have suffered from whooping cough are often sent out with the hop-pickers; they play about on the bare ground in the most careless manner, and yet recover. Air and hops are wonderful restoratives. After passing an afternoon with the drier in the kiln, seated close to a great heap of hops and inhaling the odour, I was in a condition of agreeable excitement all the evening. My mind was full of fancy, imagination, flowing with ideas; a sense of lightness and joyousness lifted me up. I wanted music, and felt full of laughter. Like the half-fabled hashish, the golden bloom of the hops had entered the nervous system; intoxication without wine, without injurious after-effect, dream intoxication; they were wine for the nerves. If hops only grew in the Far East we should think wonders of so powerful a plant. At hop-picking a girl can earn about 10/- a week, so that it is not such a highly paid employment as might be supposed from the talk there is about it. The advantages are sideways, so to say; a whole family can work at the same time, and the sum-total becomes considerable. Hopping happily comes on just after corn harvest, so that the labourers get two harvest-times. The farmers find it an expensive crop. It costs £50 or £60 to pick a very small garden, and if the Egyptian plague of insects has prevailed the price at market will not repay the expenditure. The people talk much of a possible duty on foreign hops. The hop farmer should have a ladybird on his seal ring for his sign and token, for the ladybird is his great friend. Ladybirds (and their larvae) destroy myriads of the aphids which cause rust, and a flight of ladybirds should be welcomed as much as a flight of locusts is execrated in other countries.

One of the hop-picking women told me how she went to church and the parson preached such a curious sermon, all about our 'innerds' (inwards, insides), and how many 'boanes' we had, and by and by 'he told us that we were the only beasts who had the use of our hands'. Years since at village schools the girls used to swallow pins; first one would do it, then another, presently half the school were taking pins. Ignorant of physiology! Yet they did not seem to suffer; the pins did not penetrate the pleura or lodge in the processes. Now Anatomy climbs into the pulpit and shakes a bony fist at the congregation. That is the humerus of it, as Corporal Nym might say. At the late election — the cow election — the candidates were Brown, Conservative, and Stiggins, Liberal. The day after the polling a farm labourer was asked how he filled up his voting paper. 'Oh', said he full of the promised cow, 'I doan't care for that there

Brown chap, he bean't no good; zo I jest put a cross agen he, and voted for Stiggins.' The dream of life was accomplished, the labourer had a vote, and — irony — he voted exactly opposite to his intent.

Too-whoo! ooo! — the sound of a horn — the hunt was up; but this was not the hunting season. Looking out of the kiln door I saw a boy running at full speed down the lane with a small drainpipe tucked under his arm. He stopped, put the pipe to his mouth, and blew a blast on this 'dread horn', then jumped through a gap in the hedge and disappeared. They were playing fox and hounds; who but a boy would have thought of using a drainpipe for a horn? It gave a good note, too. In and about the kiln I learned that if you smash a frog with a stone, no matter how hard you hit him, he cannot die till sunset. You must be careful not to put on any new article of clothing for the first time on a Saturday, or some severe punishment will ensue. One person put on his new boots on a Saturday, and on Monday broke his arm. Some still believe in herbs, and gather wood-betony for herb tea, or eat dandelion leaves between slices of dry toast. There is an old man living in one of the villages who has reached the age of a hundred and sixty years, and still goes hop-picking. Ever so many people had seen him and knew all about him; an undoubted fact, a public fact; but I could not trace him to his lair. His exact whereabouts could not be fixed. I live in hopes of finding him in some obscure 'Hole' yet (many little hamlets are 'Holes,' as Froghole, Foxhole). What an exhibit for London! Did he but realise his own value, he would soon come forth. I joke, but the existence of this antique person is firmly believed in. Sparrows are called 'spadgers'. The cat wandering about got caught in the rat-clams — i.e. a gin. Another cat was the miller's favourite at the windmill, a well-fed, happy, purring pussy, fond of the floury miller — he as white as snow, she as black as a coal. One day pussy was ingeniously examining the machinery, when the wind suddenly rose, the sails revolved, and she was ground up, fulfilling the ogre's threat — 'I'll grind his bones to make my bread.' This was not so sad as the fate of the innkeeper's cow. You have read the *Arabian Nights* — that book of wisdom, for in truth the stories are no stories; they are the records of ancient experience, the experience of a thousand years, and some of them are as true and as deeply to be pondered on as anything in the holiest books the world reverences. You remember the Three Calenders, each of whom lost an eye — struck out in the most arbitrary and cruel fashion. The innkeeper had a cow, a very pretty, quiet cow, but in time it came about that her left horn, turning inwards, grew in such a manner that it threatened to force the point into her head. To remedy this the top of the horn was sawn off and a brass knob fastened on the tip, as is the custom. The cow passed the summer in the meadows with the rest, till by and by it was found that she had gone blind in the left eye. It happened in this way: the rays of the sun heated the brass knob and so destroyed the sight. Unable to call attention to its suffering, the poor creature was compelled to endure, and could not escape. Now the Three Calenders could speak, and had the advantage of human intelligence, and yet each lost an eye, and they were as helpless in the hands of fate as this poor animal.

Down in one of the hamlets there was a forge to which all the workpeople who wanted any tools sharpened carried their instruments, the smith being able to put a better edge on. Other blacksmiths or carpenters, if they required a particularly good edge for some purpose, came to him. This art he had acquired from his grandfather as a sort of heirloom or secret. The grandfather while at work used to trouble and puzzle himself how to get a very sharp edge, and at length one night he dreamed how to do it. From that time he became prosperous. If a celebrated sonata was revealed in a dream, why not the way to sharpen a chisel?

When he was tired the drier said he was 'dreggy'. They were talking of the lambs, and how that dry season they had scarcely any sweetbreads. The sweetbreads were so scanty, the butchers did not even offer them for sale; the lambs had fed on dry food. In seasons when there was plenty of grass and green food they had good large sweetbreads, white as milk. The character of the food does thus under some circumstances really alter the condition of an organ. The sweetbread is the pancreas; now a deficient pancreatic action is supposed to play a great part in consumption and other wasting diseases. Have we here, then, an indication that when the pancreas may be suspected, plenty of succulent food and plenty of liquid are nature's remedies? We looked over at the pigs in the sty. They were rooting about in a mess of garbage. 'Oh, what dirty things pigs are!' said a lady. 'Yes, ma'am; they're rightly named', said he. Some scientific gentleman in the district had a large telescope with which he made frequent observations, and at times would let a labouring man look at the moon. 'Ah,' said our friend, shaking his head in a solemn, impressive way, 'my brother, he see through it; he see great rocks and seas up there. He say he never want to see through it no more. He wish he never looked through him at all.' The poor man was dreadfully frightened at what he had seen in the moon. At first I laughed at the story and the odd idea of a huge, great fellow being alarmed at a glance through a telescope. Since then, however, on reflection, it seems to me perfectly natural. He was illiterate; he had never read of astronomy; to him it was really like a sudden peep into another world, for the instrument was exceptionally powerful, and the view of the sunlight on the peaks and the shadows in the valleys must have been extraordinary to him. There was nothing to laugh at; the incident shows what a great and wonderful thing it is that rocks and mountains should be whirled along over our heads. The idea has become familiarised to us by reading, but the fact is none the less marvellous. This man saw the fact first, before he had the idea, and he had sufficient imagination to realise it. At the village post office they ask for 'Letterhead, please sir,' instead of a stamp, for it is characteristic of the cottager that whatever words he uses must be different from those employed by other people. Stamp is as familiar to him as to you, yet he prefers to say 'letterhead' — because he does. There are many curious old houses, some of them timbered, still standing in these parts. The immense hearths which were once necessary for burning wood are now occupied with 'duck's-nest' grates, so called from the bars forming a sort of nest. In one of the hamlets the women touched their hats to us.

Not far from the hop-kiln I found a place where charcoal-burning was carried on. The brown charcoal-burner, upright as a bolt, walked slowly round the smouldering heap, and wherever flame seemed inclined to

break out cast damp ashes upon the spot. Six or seven water-butts stood in a row for his use. To windward he had built a fence of flakes, or wattles as they are called here, well worked in with brushwood, to break the force of the draught along the hillside, which would have caused too fierce a fire. At one side stood his hut of poles meeting in a cone, wrapped round with rough canvas. Besides his rake and shovel and a short ladder, he showed me a tool like an immense gridiron, bent half double, and fitted to a handle in the same way as a spade. This was for sifting charcoal when burned, and separating the small from the larger pieces. Every now and then a puff of smoke rose from the heap and drifted along; it had a peculiar odour, a dense, thick smell of smothered wood coal, to me not disagreeable, but to some people so annoying that they have been known to leave their houses and abandon a locality where charcoal-burning was practised. Dim memories of old days come crowding round me, invisible to him, to me visible and alive, of the kings, great hunters, who met with the charcoal-burners in the vast forests of mediaeval days, of the noble knights and dames whom the rude charcoal-burners guided to their castles through trackless wastes, and all the romance of old. Scarcely is there a tale of knightly adventure that does not in some way or other mention these men, whose occupation fixed them in the wilderness which of yore stretched between cultivated places. I looked at the modern charcoal-burner with interest. He was brown, good-looking, upright, and distinctly superior in general style to the common run of working men. He spoke without broad accent and used correct language; he was well educated and up to the age. He knew his own mind, and had an independent expression; a very civil, intelligent, and straightforward man. No rude charcoal-burner of old days this. We stood close to the highway road; a gentleman's house was within a stone's throw; the spot, like the man, was altogether the reverse of what we read in ancient story. Yet such is the force of association that I could not even now divest myself of those dim memories and living dreams of old; there seemed as it were the clank of armour, a rustle of pennons in the leaves; it would have been quite natural to hold bow and arrow in the hand. The descent was unbroken. The charcoal-burner traced back to the Norman Conquest. That very spot where we stood, now surrounded with meadows and near dwellings, scarcely thirty years since had formed part of one of the largest of the old forests. It was forest land. Woods away on the slope still remained to witness to traditions. As the charcoal-burner worked beside the modern highway, so his trade had come down and was still practised in the midst of modern trades, in these times of sea-coal and steam. He told me that he and his brothers were maintained by charcoal-burning the year through, and, it appeared, in a very comfortable position. They only burned a small quantity here; they moved about from place to place in the woods, according as the timber was thrown. They often stopped for weeks in the woods, watching the fires all night. A great part of the work was done in the winter, beginning in October — after the hop-picking. Now resting in his lonely hut, now walking round and tending the smoking heap, the charcoal-burner watched out the long winter nights while the stars drifted over the leafless trees, till the grey dawn came with hoar-frost. He liked his office, but owned that the winter nights were very long. Starlight and frost and slow time are the same now as when the red deer and the wild boar dwelt in the forest. Much of the charcoal was prepared for hop-drying, large quantities being used for that purpose. At one time a considerable amount was rebaked for patent fuel, and the last use to which it had been put was in carrying out some process with Australian meat. It was still necessary in several trades. Goldsmiths used charcoal for soldering. They preferred the charcoal made from the thick bark of the butts of birch trees. At the foot or butt of the birch the bark grows very thick, in contrast to the rind higher, which is thinner than on other trees. Lord Sheffield's mansion at Fletching was the last great house he knew that was entirely warmed with charcoal, nothing else being burnt. Charcoal was still used in houses for heating plates. But the principal demand seemed to be for hop-drying purposes — the charcoal burned in the kiln where I had been resting was made on the spot. This heap he was now burning was all of birch poles, and would be four days and four nights completing. On the fourth morning it was drawn, and about seventy sacks were filled, the charcoal being roughly sorted.

The ancient forest land is still wild enough, there is no seeming end to the heath and fern on the ridges or to the woods in the valleys. These moor-like stretches bear a resemblance to parts of Exmoor. The oaks that once reached from here to the seashore were burned to smelt the iron in the days when Sussex was the great iron land. For charcoal the vast forests were cut down; it seems strange to think that cannon were once cast — the cannon that won India for us — where now the hops grow and the plough travels slowly, so opposite as they are to the roaring furnace and the ringing hammer. Burned and blasted by the heat, the ground where the furnaces were still retains the marks of the fire. But today there is silence; the sunshine lights up the purple heather and the already yellowing fern; the tall and beautiful larches stand graceful in the stillness. Their lines always flow in pleasant curves; they need no wind to bend them into loveliness of form: so quiet and deserted is the place that the wide highway road is green with vegetation, and the impression of our wheels is the only trace upon them. Looking up the road — up the hill — it appears green almost from side to side. It is well made and firm, and fit for any traffic; but a growth of minute weeds has sprung up, and upon these our wheels leave their marks. Of roads that have become grass-grown in war-desolated countries we have all read, but this is our own unscathed England.

The nature of the ancient forest, its quiet and untrodden silence, adheres to the site. Far down in the valley there is more stirring, and the way is well pulverised. In the hollow there is an open space, backed by the old beech trees of the park, dotted with ashes, and in the midst a farmhouse partly timbered. Here by the roadside they point out to you a low mound, at the very edge of the road, which could easily be passed unnoticed as a mere heap of scrapings overgrown with weeds and thistles. On looking closer it appears more regularly shaped; it is indeed a grave. Of old time an unfortunate women committed suicide, and according to the barbarous law of those days her body was buried at the crossroads and a stake driven through it. That was the end so far as the brutal law of the land went. But the road-menders, with better hearts, from that day to this have always kept up the mound. However beautiful the day, however beautiful the beech trees and the ashes that stand apart, there is always a melancholy feeling in passing the place. This thistle-grown mound saddens the whole, it is impossible to forget it; it lies, as it were, under everything, under the beeches, the sunlit sward and fern. The mark of death is there. The dogs and the driven cattle tread the spot; a human being has passed into dust. The circumstance of the mound having been kept up so many years bears curious testimony to the force of tradition. Many writers altogether deny the value of tradition. Dr. Schliemann's spade, however, found Troy. Perhaps tradition is like the fool of the saying, and is sometimes right.

The Manchester Guardian, 24 and 31 August 1886